JAMIE THOM

TALKING
TO TEENAGERS

A GUIDE TO SKILFUL CLASSROOM
COMMUNICATION

First published 2023

by John Catt Educational Ltd,
15 Riduna Park, Station Road,
Melton, Woodbridge IP12 1QT

Tel: +44 (0) 1394 389850
Email: enquiries@johncatt.com
Website: www.johncatt.com

ISBN: 978 1 398386 50 1

Set and designed by John Catt Educational Limited

For Matthew.

Let me communicate this very simply: you are wonderful.

CONTENTS

PREFACE

The majority of this book was written during my last year teaching in the classroom. I was balancing teaching English four days a week with looking after my two small boys.

In an attempt to maintain sanity and professional engagement when experiencing sleepless nights with a toddler and a newborn, I gave myself a pedagogical focus: what can I do to improve the way I communicate with young people? What impact will focusing carefully on my own talk and behaviour in the classroom have on honing relationships and the quality of learning in my classroom?

I wanted to examine this through the lens of five areas: understanding teenagers; using non-verbal communication effectively; being proactive in managing behaviour; improving classroom discussion; and motivating teenagers.

A book that is entitled *Talking to Teenagers* also had to include the voice of those who matter the most in this dialogue: teenagers themselves. I surveyed hundreds of teenagers from across the UK for this book, and interviewed a wide number of teenagers to get their views on classroom practice. That subjective experience was also combined with reading a wide range of research, and discussions with experts on the teenage brain and communication (both through informal interviews and interviews for my podcast: *Beyond Survival: The New Teacher Podcast*).

I have now left the classroom and started a new teacher training course for English teachers at Edinburgh Napier University. I have spent the first six months in that role reflecting on and honing the contents of this book. This, therefore, will be the last book I write at the 'chalkface': that is, writing alongside teaching a full timetable in a secondary school. I have loved going through this process of combining teaching and writing. It has deeply impacted my own classroom practice – and has hopefully in turn supported other teachers in their own work.

My initial work with new teachers has further reinforced how much teaching is a performance- and communication-based profession. New teachers need to be very clearly guided on what they say, how they say it, and how to consider the intended audience. It is also why there is a significant focus on language related to behaviour in this book – for without the capacity to manage a classroom, the reality is that learning does not happen.

The profound complexity of language use in the classroom, however, means that this exploration isn't just for new teachers. Teachers at all stages of their careers can benefit from refining and reflecting on their communication in the classroom. It is through communication, after all, that all relationships are built and all learning takes place. That simple understanding, for me, marks out the best teachers I have seen – they think deeply about what they say and how it impacts the individuals in front of them.

A note on the pronoun 'we'. As most of this book was written while I was a practising secondary school teacher, I have written in the first-person teacher voice.

I wrestled with changing that – given the fact that I am no longer in the secondary classroom on a full-time basis – and having a more dispassionate authorial voice, but I feel the book represents me writing as a classroom teacher. It also reflects my belief that I will always be a teacher, in whatever form that takes, and my profound commitment to devoting the rest of my working life to supporting the development of teachers and leaders at all stages of their careers.

I hope the contents of this book can provide some contribution to that aim.

INTRODUCTION

'How a teacher speaks to me is really important. I know if they are interested in me and care about how I learn.'

Sarah, 16, Newcastle

Teaching is communication. How we speak, how we act, and how we express ourselves in the classroom is absolutely vital. It can be the difference between building positive relationships and inspiring a deep love of learning, and a complete breakdown in how our classrooms and learning function. What we say as teachers *deeply* matters.

If anything, the elevated demands on our interpersonal skills can be one of the most exhausting parts of working in a school. We are listened to intently (ideally!) throughout the day – and we are under a significant degree of scrutiny from those in front of us. It is no exaggeration to say that under that microscope, everything we do is communication.

There are few other professions in which the levels and range of communications we are expected to have equal this intensity. The need to be clear, to be precise, and to be memorable is vital. Teaching is also a performance profession, one that requires us to script out our interactions, to prepare, to rehearse and to practise.

We are – to embrace a cliché – actors who are on stage all day, every day. We, however, have no lines to fall back on – we only have our toolbox of verbal and non-verbal skills. Our success in the classroom lies in our capacity to skilfully judge a moment and use our communication skills to their best effect. Not only do we have to communicate to ensure learning, but we also have to do so in order to build effective relationships – the two are synonymous in the classroom: without either one, there will be no learning.

The fact that in the secondary school context there is a strangely segmented environment, with lessons changing as rapidly as every 45 minutes, means that communication is given not only an added complexity, but also an added urgency. We don't have the luxury of time to make how we talk have more impact – we have to package it all neatly in an attempt to secure learning in the time allocated.

It is often that ability to communicate effectively that can mark us out as memorable teachers – the teachers that have an impact on others, as Willingham states in *Why Don't Students Like School?*:

> 'Ask ten people you know 'Who was the most important teacher in your life?'. I've asked dozens of people this question and have noticed two interesting things. First, most people have a ready answer. Second, the reason that one teacher made a strong impression is almost always emotional. The reasons are never things like "she taught me a lot of math." People say things like "she made me believe in myself" or "she taught me to love knowledge."'

How do we generate that emotional response? Through what humanistic psychologist Carl Rogers would define as our 'way of being', which very simply is an expression of how we communicate.

Interpersonal skills

I have been fortunate to work in schools with brilliant teachers and leaders across the UK: from central London, to coastal schools in the North-East of England, to schools in Scotland.

The very best educators are not homogenous but they all share one commonality: they are superb communicators with outstanding interpersonal skills. They connect with people on an individual basis, they can diffuse conflicts quickly and they are superb listeners.

Part of the mission of this book is to try to discover their secrets; to slowly grow and develop in our own communication so that we can forge similarly transformative relationships with teenagers in classrooms.

The time conundrum

Despite this endless classroom dialogue, there never seems to be enough time for us teachers to really consider how we speak and what impact it can have on the young people in front of us. The reality is that this aspect of teacher reflection is vitally important: how do we know if our communication is effective? It does not, after all, exist in a vacuum. It is about how it is received by those in front of us. As I write this book, to consider an example, I am reflecting carefully on the intended audience – teachers of teenagers – and thus adapting my writing as it progresses. That consideration will be, hopefully, what enables me to find some clarity and impact in my words.

Classroom teachers' lives are dictated by school bells – by communication that exists on autopilot. By the nature of our jobs, our communication is often *mindless*, rather than reflective, considered and impactful. The aim of this book is to change that, and to give busy teachers the space to pause and break down all the layers of teacher communication, and to consider how we refine those skills in order to use them to achieve their full potential. In doing so, its intention is to leave readers with a range of strategies that will drive forward relationships, learning and our impact in the classroom.

With short reflective pieces on each particular area of communication, this book aims to be a practical one that teachers can come back to again and again.

Language

As an English teacher, I place huge value on the power and impact of both the spoken and written word. I am keenly aware of just how much influence it can have in the public arena. Recent political developments across the world mark this out with complete clarity. I am also the father of two small children, and recognise how much we influence them as communicators as they begin their own adventures with building language.

Teaching is one of the few professions that, if we found ourselves transported back 100 years, we would find the scenario comfortingly familiar. There would be a teacher communicating with young people, there would be dialogue – there would be an atmosphere of thinking.

Communication involves the transference between an individual and a receiver. Another reason why secondary teaching is challenging is the nature of the audience: the oft demonised teenager. What better place to start than to devote some time to reflecting on our adolescent audiences. Who are they? What preconceptions do they bring? Why do some of them strongly dislike school?

— PART ONE —

UNDERSTAND THE COMPLEXITY OF THE TEENAGE AUDIENCE

'I would there were no age between ten and three-and-twenty, or that youth would sleep out the rest; for there is nothing in the between but getting wenches with child, wronging the ancientry, stealing, fighting.'

William Shakespeare, *The Winter's Tale*

TEEN TALK

What do you think are the hardest things about being a teenager?

'Coping up with the sudden pressure and responsibilities that arrive when you become a teenager.'

'The pressure from school, and other teenagers around us.'

'Adults expecting us to act like adults yet treating us like children – double standards.'

'Lack of understanding from (what feels like) everyone around you.'

'The behaviour of others: unlike others, I do not wear designer clothes, or go out only to do silly things (such as throw rocks at buses), play sports, etc. It's so annoying reading about people calling us teens idiots despite the fact there are some good ones out there! Really not a fan of the toxicity among a lot of teens too, especially those who use Snapchat and may bully people on there or take photographs without prior permission.'

'All the pressures such as pressure to become someone you're not in order to fit in at school and in society.'

'I think nobody takes you seriously.'

'People not understanding or listening or accepting your choices.'

'Making life decisions that could make a big impact on my future.'

'Being able to be good at it all. You need to learn that it's not possible to be great at everything and every test.'

'Separating own opinions and sense of self from that of friends.'

'One of the most challenging things about being a teenager is taking in/ remembering information like how to answer exam-style questions or difficult tasks.'

'When you begin to realise that you are growing up and maturing, when you notice that the world around you soon won't just let someone hold your hand through everything that you do. Without knowing, without truly understanding the world, we are about to be shoved into it. That's terrifying, but everyone does it.'

'The overarching feeling of dread that looms over one's head. Where will I be in the future? When will I die? What if I don't make it? What is everything, why is everything? Just, what?'

'Dealing with your mental health and having no one listen to you. All while having to do homework or extracurriculars. Not being able to talk freely.'

'It depends on what you're going through. For me it is communicating when I need help – I seem to be incapable of doing so sometimes. It isn't just a puberty thing, it's been that way my whole life, but being a teenager doesn't help, because people assume that you can deal with your issues on your own.'

'The most challenging thing about being a teenager is juggling responsibilities like school, as well as distractions like video games, while also trying to learn about yourself and figure out what type of person you are.'

'Low self-esteem, comparing yourself with others.'

'After maturing from being an irresponsible annoying child you're forced into high school and have to figure out everything about yourself. I think the hardest thing about being a teenager is trying to find who you are, your interests, your sexuality, your gender identity. Then on top of that it feels like you only have a short amount of time to do so before you have to sell yourself, convincing universities that you're interesting, developed and worth their time. It's so much pressure for a teenager like me who just wants to read books and tell dumb jokes, not think about my entire future.'

'The fact that your parents always expect you to be the best or more mature because you are a teenager. You are expected to clean the house, help with the kids, be mature and just have your entire childhood taken away just because you reached a certain age.'

'I think the most challenging thing about being a teenager is the pressure. The pressure to be a certain type of person from family and teachers, the pressure to consistently achieve, the peer pressure from friends to explore new avenues, and most of all, the pressure from within to conform and to live up to these expectations.'

'Your teenage years are a time for self-discovery, but it is difficult to do when you have different expectations and pressures suffocating you.'

'Hormones and acne!'

'The things that you are thinking about, and what you want to be, are not same as your dad or mum.'

'The confusion of figuring out who you are, where you stand and what you want. In education the idea of having set goals and plans post-16 is drilled into us. However, many of us don't actually know what we want… Teenagers are faced with life-changing decisions and moments all throughout secondary school and post-16 education, and ultimately, life is about more than working, and unfortunately this is not being spoken about in schools and this has created, in my opinion, a toxic environment where teenagers feel pressured to commit and make their mind up about the rest of their life, the moment they turn 13.'

'A constant feeling of being overwhelmed, but also really wanting to fit in.'

'Constant stress over falling out with your friends, particularly on social media.'

'No one really knows what you're thinking and they just assume things about how you are feeling, or what you want to do.'

'Being a teenager made me realise that life is not as simple as I thought. When I was a kid, it was much less complicated and pressurised. Another problem is that when I have exams, I am worried about being judged by others, so I can't focus. When the exams eventually come, I am frustrated that I don't get the mark that I want because of not being able to focus.'

ON THE OUTSIDE

'I'm on the outside, I'm looking in
I can see through you, see your true colours
'Cause inside you're ugly, you're ugly like me
I can see through you, see to the real you.'

Staind, 'Outside'

I was a music obsessive as a child (and I still very much am). I now consider most of my young taste to have been acceptable, even 'cool' – and I am now working hard to persuade my own children to appreciate some of my finer band choices. When my four-year-old asked in the car the other day, 'Daddy, please can we listen to Oasis', I felt a fatherly pride that had never before been matched.

From the ages of around 13 to 16, however, I went through a rather dark obsession with angry and loud metal music. The delightfully named, and quoted above, Staind were one of my favourites (alongside similarly quaint names like Slipknot, System of a Down, Deftones and many others). Long hair, long hoodies and a long grunting attitude to most aspects of life quickly followed.

As we shall see is a ubiquitous feature of teenage behaviour, the principal reason for my descent into the darkness of metal music was peer norms. All my friends and most of my year group (certainly the 'cool' teenagers) had become obsessed with metal music.

Despite this strong societal pull to 'fit in', I often did feel that I was 'on the outside', though it is a stretch to imply that I defined myself as a 'stain' as a teenager, since I was a shy and probably fairly sensitive chap (not that

I would admit it at the time). If social media had been around, goodness knows what sort of overly emotive, self-absorbed stuff I would have put out into the world.

I also certainly felt the tug of both the societal and parental 'pressure' and the overwhelming sense of confusion that is clear in the teenagers' responses that open this chapter. I am not alone in that descent into a tendency towards self-absorption that marks the teenage years. This letter printed in *The Guardian* (Hall, 2013) is a particularly good, and funny, example of the centrality of this particular teenager's experience over anything else:

> 'There's nothing like teenage diaries for putting momentous historical events in perspective (Banalities and bathos, 31 December). This is my entry for 20 July 1969. "I went to arts centre (by myself!) in yellow cords and blouse. Ian was there but he didn't speak to me. Got a rhyme put in my handbag from someone who's apparently got a crush on me. It's Nicholas, I think. UGH. Man landed on moon." **Dinah Hall**, Lustleigh, Devon.'

Challenges

Of course, not all teenagers manifest such comic levels of narcissism or indeed obvious degrees of insecurity.

To argue that teenagers are homogenous would be to do them a great disservice – and cause any teacher to snort with knowing derision. Spend a lesson with any group of teenagers and you will see that they are as diverse as any groups of adults: the extroverts, the introverts, the hard-working, the lazy, the polite, the rude – the list of opposites is as endless as it is rich.

This process of reflection on your own experience as a teenager is important in fostering empathy for just how challenging it is for the individuals who grace our classrooms every day. The next fuel for empathy, which we will shortly explore, is delving into some of the fascinating research about how the teenage brain functions. After all, we cannot communicate effectively with any audience unless we endeavour to understand and appreciate them and their context.

Dr John Coleman, the author of many books on teenagers and whom I interviewed in preparation for this book, captures the intense scope of this period of development in his essay 'Why I Study Adolescence' (Coleman, 2022).

> 'From child to adult, the adolescent period represents one of the greatest psychological transitions we experience.'

Given the fact that we spent all day in their company, having some sense of practical understanding of this profound scope of change will help us to communicate with them more effectively.

When does adolescence begin?

To answer this, let's return to Dr Coleman (2011) in his seminal work *The Nature of Adolescence.*

> 'What exactly is adolescence? For many people this stage of life is a puzzle. To begin with it is far from clear when the stage starts, and when it ends. Where do the boundaries of adolescence lie? Does it start at puberty and end at age 20? Is this too simplistic? For some, the age of 13 is a good starting point, yet what might be understood as adolescent behaviour can be seen at an earlier age, and today many believe that young adults who still live at home in their early twenties are to all intents and purposes adolescents.'

Regardless of the boundaries of adolescence, one commonality of teenagers during this period is a desire to create an authentic sense of self. In the fascinating *Inventing Ourselves: The Secret Life of the Teenage Brain*, Sarah-Jayne Blakemore captures this particularly well:

> 'During adolescence, your sense of who you are – your moral and political beliefs, your music and fashion tastes, what social group you associate with – undergoes profound change. During adolescence, we are inventing ourselves.'

Our audience

Those individuals going through such significant change are present in our classrooms every day: they are our audience. While the purpose of this section of the book is not to add fuel to the relentless negativity that surrounds teenagers, it will give some reasons (note, not excuses) as to why some teenagers can find it challenging to be in our classrooms.

23

The rationale for starting this book with an exploration of teenagers is very simple: our capacity to understand the experience and inner lives of teenagers is profoundly influential in determining whether or not they learn anything in our company.

It might sound trite, but the words of empathetic wisdom that Atticus passes on to his young daughter Scout in *To Kill a Mockingbird* should be reflected on by anyone who spends their working day in the company of teenagers:

> 'You never really understand a person until you consider things from his point of view... until you climb in his skin and walk around in it.'

What we shall see in the next chapter, however, is that teenagers are often unfairly maligned and criticised by society – not the recipients of as much understanding and compassion as we might hope.

NEGATIVITY

If we surveyed 100 adults on their perceptions of teenagers, what would we discover? While it would be unfair to suggest there would be universal disapproval, we only need to glance at how the media often demonises teenagers; or observe people crossing the road to avoid groups of teenagers; or eaves drop on parents of teenagers expressing their frustration, to question if the survey observations would be entirely positive.

There is nothing new in this. We can go all the way back to Socrates, somewhere around 469 BC, to understand that young people have always vilified.

> 'Children; they have bad manners, contempt for authority; they show disrespect for elders and love chatter in place of exercise. They no longer rise when elders enter the room, they contradict their parents and tyrannize their teachers. Children are now tyrants.'

'Tyrannize their teachers' is an expression that I am sure sounds familiar, an accusation that teenagers are often tarred with. Such harsh views are expressed even more succinctly by the French writer Anaïs Nin: 'Adolescence is like a cactus.' (Anaïs Nin, *Solar Barque*, 1958.) The implications of this are clear: spiky, painful and not particularly attractive!

These cultural stereotypes can reinforce the view that teenagers have of themselves as outsiders – and can be a self-fulfilling prophecy that adds fuel to teenagers behaving in challenging ways. Glancing at the pages of one of the most famous of teenage diary writers, Anne Frank, we can see plenty of evidence of this:

> 'If I talk everyone thinks I am showing off, when I am silent they think I am ridiculous: rude if I answer back, sly if I get an idea,

lazy if I'm tired, selfish if I eat a mouthful more than I should, stupid, cowardly, crafty etc, etc, etc.'

If we consider how we feel as teachers when we are labelled with relentless negativity, it helps to give us some sense of how it must feel to be a teenager in the face of such hostility. Remember the headlines about 'lazy teachers' during the coronavirus pandemic?

Apathy towards school

That societal negativity could perhaps be one reason why lots of teenagers feel a sense of apathy towards school. Indeed, one of the most significant challenges we face with our teenage audience is that often it comes with a sense of frustration and dislike of school. Their lives are very much dictated by their experience of school: they spend more waking time in school than in any other context. There is no autonomy involved; they are forced to be in our company every day.

This is why striving to build an inclusive environment in which teenagers feel some sense of community and engagement with school is so vital: like all of us, they have a need to feel engaged and accepted in an environment they spend such a significant amount of time in.

Again, it is important to clarify this isn't every teenager in the land – some teenagers absolutely thrive in the school environment. Later, we will also look in more detail at ways in which we can communicate to challenge some of that thinking. We are, after all, agents in this process: we can have a profound influence on how positively or negatively teenagers feel about our subjects and school in general. To illuminate this point further, just ask any adult who their favourite teacher was; the answer is often offered immediately, and it is fascinating to see how it often relates to a choice in further study or profession.

So where does that teenage apathy towards school generate from? Clearly there are peer relationships that influence it: it is never going to be particularly 'cool' to passionately declare your love of learning at all levels.

There is also the scale of competing attention that now exists for teenagers – social media, video games, etc. – all of which appeal to the extensive dopamine (reward hormone) that is floating around in the teenage brain, which means that we are facing an uphill battle in terms of immediacy.

The thinking struggle

In *Why Don't Students Like School?*, cognitive scientist Daniel Willingham also makes it very clear how challenging the process of learning is for teenagers.

> 'Contrary to popular belief, the brain is not designed for thinking. It's designed to save you from having to think, because the brain is actually not very good at thinking. Thinking is slow and unreliable...'

He concludes this by suggesting 'people ... are not naturally good thinkers; unless the cognitive conditions are right, we will avoid thinking'.

Now, given the immense internal challenges that teenagers are experiencing, any attempt to secure cognitive conditions that will aid their learning becomes even more important. The reality is that teenagers' extensive brain development means that often those 'cognitive conditions' are very challenging to secure.

A new narrative

Part of our classroom aims should be about challenging negativity towards teenagers: we should be striving to create new 'stories' about what teenagers are like, and the various qualities and accomplishments that they can – and do – contribute to our society.

This needs to be explicit: we need to make sure that we carefully plan how we give them marked opportunities to demonstrate their wonderful qualities. These opportunities can range from simple, everyday acts such as embracing laughter (this can play a vital role), to those that are more strategic, such as encouraging teenagers to take part in charity projects or connect with the wider environment.

Discussing the research into the teenage brain with teenagers can also be very beneficial, helping them to understand their behaviour and that of their peers. It can also help them to feel less ostracised to see that the teenage years are challenging for anyone who has to undertake them.

It is simple and easy to fall into complaining and berating teenagers – they can, after all, be infuriating – but our presence in the classroom will be so much more positive and compassionate if we try to avoid such lazy stereotyping. As a parent of two very young children, I know what superhuman patience it requires of me, and how the drive for my attempts at this often comes from the understanding that their brains and emotions are undergoing significant development. Not to be patronising to teenagers, but that sense of deep empathy, compassion and patience also needs to be at the core of how we interact with teenagers. It also allows us to move away from some of the unhelpful myths that surround adolescence development: that they are lazy, that they are immature and their hormones are just raging. None of these oversimplistic definitions will help us be better teachers for them – if anything, it will just leave them feeling even more misunderstood.

Luckily for us, there has been significant research in the past 20 years about the teenage brain, with some fascinating discoveries that provide some clarity on why teenagers behave in the ways that they do and that might just stop society being so quick to demonise them.

THE TEENAGE BRAIN

In the contexts of our lessons, our teenage audience's brains are, of course, remarkably important. We need them to demonstrate unnatural powers of concentration (do you attend six or seven mini-lecture-style events every day?), be receptive and engaged in dialogue and discussions, and then often to retain that information for stressful examination-style situations months later.

While that seems obvious, have we ever really invested careful reflection about what happens inside those brains we are investing such energy in? Without this attempt to understand the maturation and development of the teenagers that make up our classrooms, we are effectively working in the dark. Teaching is far too important to allow for guess work, which is why this chapter is vital in our discourse of how to improve communication with teenagers.

New insights

For a long time, society believed that teenagers behaved in the way they did merely because of what G. Stanley Hall, who coined the term adolescence, described in 1904 as 'the storm and stress' of this time. That 'storm and stress' was often attributed to hormones and external social factors.

As Sarah-Jayne Blakemore highlights in *Inventing Ourselves: The Secret Life of the Teenage Brain*, our understanding now has now changed profoundly:

> 'Contrary to the received wisdom up to the late twentieth century, we now know that our brains are dynamic and constantly changing into adulthood, and the transformation they undergo in early life continues for far longer and has much bigger implications than

was previously thought. Modern brain-scanning technology like magnetic resonance imaging (MRI) is ushering in a new era of understanding of the physiological mechanisms that underpin our sense of who we are, the sense of self that develops during adolescence.'

So what have MRI scans revealed about the teenage brain?

Difference

One thing we need to be conscious of is the fact that adult and teenage brains work in markedly different ways. During adolescence there is a huge amount of brain maturation going on, with the brain effectively going through a restructuring process. There is also a significant difference in terms of the plasticity elements of the brain, implying teenagers are better at changing, adapting and responding to the environment.

We wonderful rational adults (cough) think with our prefrontal cortex: the part of the brain that uses judgement and makes us aware of long-term consequences. Teens, on the other hand, process information with the amygdala, which is the part of the brain that deals with our emotions. Teens consequently feel much more than they think. Not wonderfully helpful for us as teachers when our role is to inspire thinking in them. Their prefrontal cortices are in a state of profound flux. We will explore the reason for this shortly.

Again, anyone who spends time in a classroom will be able to testify to this, but the connection in the teenage brain between the emotion and the decision-making centre is still developing. That is why, at times, their choices and behaviour can be remarkably challenging to understand. It also goes some way in explaining why there can be a perplexing contrast between moments of maturity and illogical and impulsive behaviour.

While clearly it can cause friction in our relationships with them, and explain some of the volatility we see in classroom settings, it is also challenging for teenagers. This activity in the brain can provide some justification for the mood swings and conflict we can at times see from teenagers.

Pruning

When I interviewed Dr John Coleman about the teenage brain, he had an excellent analogy for explaining the pruning process that occurs in teenagers' brains, arguing it is the brain's method for becoming a 'leaner, fitter, fighting machine'. Fundamentally, the pruning process is what makes a teenager's brain more efficient.

What effectively happens is that many unused connections that are part of a child's brain are 'pruned' away in adolescence. Scientists call this process 'synaptic pruning', and argue that the brain decides which neural links to keep based on how frequently they are used.

The main change is that **unused connections in the thinking and processing part of a child's brain (called the grey matter) are 'pruned' away**. At the same time, other connections are strengthened. This is the brain's way of becoming more efficient, based on the 'use it or lose it' principle. That pruning process, however, can also influence teenage behaviour. Dan Siegel expands on this in *Brainstorm*:

> 'When adolescent pruning occurs in the integrated circuitry between hippocampus, which is important in storing memories; the corpus callosum, which links the left and right hemispheres of the brain; in the prefrontal cortex, these change, and have a profound effect on our decision-making abilities, self-regulatory processes, attention, emotional regulation, thoughts, and behavior.'

Hormones

Hormones are frequently associated with teenagers – how often have we heard the term 'raging hormones' to seek to justify teenage behaviour? What has become clearer in recent developments in understanding teenage brain development, is that the tentative balance of hormones for teenagers also impacts the brain development. The impact of this is that emotional regulation can be much more challenging for teenagers.

When I interviewed Dr John Coleman, he spoke at length about the levels of the hormones serotonin and cortisol in teenagers. Excessive cortisol results in increased levels of anxiety, while serotonin seeks to moderate anxiety. A constant battle between the two can be another factor in contributing to behaviour that often seems irrational. Finally he highlighted the excessive dopamine:

> 'Lastly it is important to mention dopamine. This is a hormone which is released when we get pleasure or enjoyment from an activity. The brain is particularly sensitive to dopamine during the teenage years, and some risky or thrill-seeking behaviours can be explained by increased dopamine activity at this time.'

Teenagers, of course, do engage in risky behaviour, particularly when encouraged to do so by their peers. This is embodied in the following anonymous quote:

> 'It seems like people accept you more if you're, like, a dangerous driver or something. If there is a line of cars going down the road and the other lane is clear and you pass eight cars at once, everybody likes that. … If my friends are with me in the car, or if there are a lot of people in the line, I would do it, but if I'm by myself and I didn't know anybody, then I wouldn't do it. That's no fun.' – Anonymous teenager, as quoted in *The Culture of Adolescent Risk-Taking* (Lightfoot, 1997, p. 10)

This is linked again to the reward system in teenagers – they are effectively being validated and rewarded for this type of behaviour by their peers. As Laurence Steinberg, a leading expert on adolescence, has argued, this might be because the area of the brain that processes reward is hypersensitive in adolescents, and the area that inhibits risky behaviour is not yet fully mature (Steinberg, 2012).

Expectations

Are our expectations of teenagers' maturity levels and capacity to cope with life too high? That is the central argument of Frances E. Jensen, the author of *The Teenage Brain*, who suggests that our expectations of teenage behaviour are often disproportionate: 'We expect a little bit more out of adolescents than we should, given where their brains are.'

These changes in the teenage brain are combined with a range of other areas of their lives that are markedly changing. The first is the remarkable voyage of self-discovery that a young person goes through while they grace the walls of a secondary school. As they go through this process, they are desperately trying to uncover more about themselves and their relationship with the world.

SELF-DISCOVERY AND PUBERTY

Let us consider a student as they enter S1 or Year 7 in a school in Britain. They are at the age of 11 or 12: essentially, still a child. Anyone who has taught those induction lessons – or indeed the first few weeks with a new class at this age – as children experience the excitement of secondary school, understands this. These 'children' are, for the most part, delightfully uninhibited – full of the passion and verve for learning that marks out the walls of primary schools. To take a somewhat pessimistic view of their secondary career development, that learning then slowly becomes more constrained and more correlated to mark schemes and the tools necessary to reach the qualifications that loom over them.

By the time they have reached S3 or Year 9, that 11-year-old's own developmental change is remarkable. The classic Harry Enfield sketch that involves Kevin counting down to the moment to when he turns 13 is a great example of this. His excitement about turning 13 quickly descends into monosyllabic grunting and heightened emotional reactions to his parents: 'I can't do anything anymore!'

While it is clearly exaggerated to comic effect, as teachers we are given a vivid insight into this developmental change. In my first school in London I was fortunate enough to keep a wonderful Year 7 class until they sat their English language GCSE at the end of Year 10. It was amazing how those young people changed and grew during that time period (despite the fact that they were subjected to far too much time with me!).

Those changes can be split into two discrete aspects: the dramatic physical changes that occur and the deepening of their internal desire to understand themselves.

Puberty

If we want to identify some of the potential triggers that can make adolescence more challenging for teenagers, then clearly puberty is going to be one. Puberty heralds a period of brain development only matched by that during infancy.

In the article 'The role of puberty in the developing adolescent brain', authors Sarah-Jayne Blakemore, Stephanie Burnett and Ronald E. Dahl, identify:

> 'The beginning of adolescence is loosely anchored to the onset of puberty, which brings dramatic alterations in hormone levels and a number of consequent physical changes. Puberty onset is also associated with profound changes in drives, motivations, psychology, and social life; these changes continue throughout adolescence.'

This is important in that it highlights the challenging and potentially overwhelming correlation for teenagers between the physical changes and the emotional changes. This may add to feelings of uncertainty they will be experiencing concerning their identities. Naturally this will also lead to mood swings, as they will alternate between wanting independence and wanting support from their parents. There is a fine balance we need to strike in our classrooms that will meet both this need for independence and the need to be treated as a young adult, with the scaffolding and support that will help teenagers feel safe.

There is also great variation as to when puberty hits, with the body growing at different rates. This can make things awkward and challenging with peer dynamics and relationships. Dr John Coleman (2011) writes in depth on this:

> 'The body alters radically in shape and size, and it is not surprising that many young adolescents experience a period of clumsiness and self-consciousness as they attempt to adapt to these changes. The body also alters in function, and new and sometimes worrying physical experiences, such as the girl's first period, or the boy's first wet dream, have to be understood. Because these things are difficult to talk about, there is perhaps too little recognition of the anxieties that are common during this stage.'

Clearly one way in which we as teachers can assist with this is by having a consistent and whole-school approach to puberty education in the curriculum. It needs to be one where teenagers feel they have people they can speak to throughout the school about challenges they might be facing. Obviously, that requires a balance of both sensitivity and knowledge in our interactions with teenagers.

Who am I?

That age-old question 'who am I?' is one that teenagers will start to explore and evaluate for the first time. The excellently named developmental psychologist Erik Erikson (who interestingly was initially a teacher) argues that in their attempts to establish a self, there is much experimenting in the teenage years as they seek to form a strong identity. That identity might take on many initial roles as they try to find something that fits. This, he suggests, is a highly cognitive and social process, which takes signals from both environment and others in order to make decisions (Benson and Bundick, 2015). During the teenage years, this process is particularly intense.

If the experience of my nieces and nephews is typical, young people's arrival in secondary school is often their passport to attaining a mobile phone (unless I am being woefully naive in this estimation!). That technology clearly will impact and influence much of their newfound voyage into self-discovery – and makes that process of finding their own identity particularly challenging. As Erikson points out, teenagers need 'freedom to choose, but not so much freedom that they cannot, in fact, choose'. Their access to the minefield that is social media can make that forging of individual identity more challenging.

Just reading about the profound changes that teenagers go through is exhausting; for teenagers themselves this can cause strain. The fact that sleep can also often be a challenge for them adds to the difficulty.

SLEEP

'I'm just too tired, sir!' It is one of the most common classroom complaints, usually uttered by a teenager slumped over the classroom chair, their bleary eyes struggling to stay open. The problem compounds itself when at this point all we have asked them to do is take off their school bag. The next 50 minutes of wrestling with quadratic equations might prove to be the real test!

The question for us has to be, is this a genuine statement? Are teenagers really as completely exhausted as they claim to be? If so, can we do anything about it? The answer is a tentative 'perhaps' – there is evidence to support their emotive claim, but where does the responsibility for this tiredness lie? The deeply cynical among us will point out that a number of teenagers lead hugely unregulated sleep lives: some are bound to their mobile phones until the small hours; some are engaging in some murderous rampage on the latest PlayStation craze; and some are watching YouTube videos about cats on repeat.

In short, some of the sleep complaints we are likely to get from teenagers are likely to self-imposed. Regardless of the reason for the sleep issues, the reality is that it is a serious issue in classrooms in which exhausted teenagers struggle to engage with learning.

Sleep deprivation consequences

There is a common consensus that teenagers do, in fact, need more sleep. The recommended amount of sleep for teenagers from the Sleep Foundation (2022a) is between eight and 10 hours of sleep a night. You don't need to be a researcher, or indeed a teacher, to know that most adolescents do not get this amount of sleep.

If we consider any day in which we have had a lack of sleep, we can understand exactly what it does to our capacity to be at our best. Currently, my teething baby means that my mind is fully sleep-deprived as I write this: my concentration is fragmented; I am less motivated and productive than on a 'normal' day; and my anxiety levels are heightened.

So, what is impacting their sleep? Arming ourselves with this knowledge will do two things. One, it will help us to understand them more. Two, it will allow us to support them, to offer them evidence-informed ways in which they can improve their sleep and, if necessary, to adapt some of our teaching to make sure we are getting the best out of them.

Night owls

It is perhaps the most common of the teenage stereotypes: the young person who stays up all night and arises from their 'pit' deep in the afternoon. It is, clearly, a sleeping pattern that is hardly conducive to the earlier and earlier school day starts. So why do teenagers do it?

According to the Sleep Foundation (2022a), teens' disposition to becoming 'night owls' is biological. Their bodies take longer to begin producing melatonin, the hormone that helps promote sleep. The reality is that they just don't start to feel tired until a later point in the day. This even has a name: delayed sleep phase syndrome. The circadian rhythm is the synchronisation of the body's functions to the natural light-dark cycle. It helps to coordinate our periods of sleep to the night-time.

So, what does this mean for teachers? In reality it means we should be discerning about what we are asking teenagers to do first thing in the morning. Setting a test at 9.00am, for example, would be counter-intuitive. When I interviewed Dr John Coleman, he called this 'a moral, even human-rights issue', and that we should plan out what we do with teenagers carefully according to what time of the school day it is.

Having a way to ease teenagers into the first lessons of the day would be helpful. Even thinking about how these early lessons might encompass some sort of movement or group work will help to 'wake up' our teenage customers, and improve the oxygen flow to the brain. Teenage yoga first thing in the morning, however, might be a step too far.

Electronic devices

There is no denying that teenagers spend a huge amount of time on electronic devices.

What is perhaps impacting teenagers' sleep most with this, however, is identified by the Sleep Foundation (2022b):

> 'Smartphones, tablets, computers, television screens, and some e-readers give off short-wavelength blue light that is very similar to sunlight. Not only does this light make us more alert, it also deceives the body into thinking it's still daytime.'

This trick of the mind that can keep teenagers awake, also coupled with increased alertness, can also be caused by engaging in cortisol-spiking activities such as video games or social media. There are also connections between excessive mobile phone and screen usage and symptoms of depression and anxiety – all of which will detrimentally impact sleep quality (Hunley, 2017). Both lead to an over-aroused mind, making it very challenging to switch off. We have already seen how sensitive to rewards teenagers' brains are, so these games are fuelling that addictive need.

An interesting research project in Norway identified that the amount of time spent on electronic devices for teenagers aged 16–19 did profoundly impact their sleep:

> 'Adolescents spent a large amount of time during the day and at bedtime using electronic devices. Daytime and bedtime use of electronic devices were both related to sleep measures, with an increased risk of short sleep duration, long sleep onset latency and increased sleep deficiency.' (Hysing et al., 2015)

It is not just electronic devices or televisions that can eat into teenagers' sleep time – some teenagers have hectic schedules that can leave them feeling frazzled and unable to unwind.

Solutions

This chapter has identified that sleep deprivation can have a seriously detrimental impact on the qualities we are trying to cultivate in teenagers. Its connection with academic performance is also clear – a lack of sleep will mean that it is challenging to pay attention and be enthusiastic about learning. A lack of sleep will also impact attendance – young people who are not getting enough sleep will be much more likely to miss time at school. Anyone who is involved in managing school attendance will also point out how often teenagers are late to school and miss vital learning at the start of the day.

Again, clearly it might be overstepping some boundaries if we become a human alarm clock and technological gatekeeper for all our students. What we can do, however, is talk about the benefits of good sleep hygiene. A school-wide approach to this is very helpful – one that is discussed during tutor time, PSHE and in our own lessons.

This clarity across the school can be achieved if we repeat the following three points:

1. Put away all electronic devices at least an hour before going to bed – don't have them in your room. Instead, build in some time for calming the mind: perhaps a bath or a good book.

2. Try to practise consistency in sleep habits – go to bed and wake up at roughly the same time. Make sure your bedroom is dark and comfortable.

3. Try to cut down on stimulants throughout the day: energy drinks, coffee, fizzy drinks, etc. Do this especially in the evening, and reach for a delightful cup of peppermint tea instead!

That said, we should proactively communicate with teenagers in our classes (and indeed keep communication channels open with their parents) if they do appear to be exhausted. We need them to be clear on what impact it has on their learning. That doesn't need to be by roaring at them in rage about the fact that they appear to be nodding off during our Shakespeare lesson. It can be done sensitively and quietly:

'I've noticed you look really tired. What time are you getting to bed?'

'Ahmed, you look really tired. Is everything OK?'

'I'm a bit worried about you, Beth. How much sleep did you get last night?'

Doing this away from peers is important, as often teenagers can wear their lack of sleep like a badge of honour, loudly showing off to their chums that they 'have been up all night on TikTok'. Removing the audience means we are more able to focus on our concerns about them as individuals and their learning.

If all else fails we can channel Shakespeare and ominously quote *Macbeth* to them: 'You lack the season of all natures, sleep.' We all know what that chronic lack of sleep did to our hero Macbeth and our heroine Lady Macbeth! We also know that Macbeth's insecurity might also be another teenage trait that we need to reflect on carefully.

INSECURITY

It doesn't take a psychologist to recognise that one reason for my teenage self-seeking escapism in the words of angry, middle-aged metal bands was a lingering sense of insecurity. It also goes without saying that as adults we can see that teenagers are often wading through a dark and prolonged 'tunnel of me'. That self-interest, of course, can make it challenging to empathise with the experience of others.

In an experiment, Sarah-Jayne Blakemore (2018) asked 112 participants (aged from 8 to 37) to make decisions about other people's welfare and timed how long it took them to respond. The questions she asked included: 'How would your friend feel if she wasn't invited to your party?' Her results showed that the response time was shorter when the participants aged, revealing that as the participants grew in age, so did their ability to empathise with others.

For teenagers this overt insecurity is entirely natural: their brains, bodies and futures are rapidly changing by the minute. They have to focus internally in order to survive this extensive change, and come out the other side unscathed. That internal insecurity is now significantly multiplied by a range of external factors: societal factors, familial pressure, relationships with peers and social media being the most obvious. The fact that the teenage years mark such a shift can also mean those internal ruminations are not always shallow and superficial, but can run deeper, with teens questioning their position in society and the perceptions that society has of them.

Those insecurities can manifest in our classrooms many ways: distractions in lessons, attention-seeking behaviours, and a general lack of engagement with school. There is also the frustration that teenagers will feel: they are not adults, yet they are attempting to mature and emulate the behaviour of adults.

Our sphere of influence

There isn't much we can explicitly do in our position as their teacher to fix these natural insecurities, nor is it part of our professional responsibility. Our relationships are built with them through the quality of the learning in our classrooms and our desire to make sure that we are teaching them effectively. There is a significant amount we can implicitly achieve, however.

We need to be conscious of how we can provide a calm contrast to the internal 'washing machine' that adolescents may be experiencing. Routines in lessons, which we will explore later, are a powerful way to achieve this state of calm. It can help for a teenager to know what they should be expecting when they enter your classroom, rather than a loose structure that can result in a lack of focus.

The clarity of our 'way of being' – a sense of continuity in our own personal behaviours and actions – is also vital, so young people know who they are going to be faced with as they enter a classroom. We can also help them to feel part of a community – a community in our classroom and their school in general that is going to help them feel connected to the learning. This is essential in seeking to encourage a more holistic perspective from teenagers, to help them to appreciate that they are part of a wider network of support.

As we shall see later, there also needs to be a sense of demarcation between the challenges that teens face outside the classroom with our reality inside it. Some space for solitude and silence, away from their challenges, can help to make this clear.

There is sense in drawing some appropriate attention to the internal struggles of teenagers – being transparent about how we manage insecurity, stress and anxiety, and being open about our own struggles as a teenager. Talking about other students we have taught and their approach to things, and building this into the curriculum, can also be helpful.

Self-control

One thing that some teenagers find challenging is self-control. Clearly, for anyone to flourish, this is an essential life skill connected to discipline and willpower.

Angela Duckworth, author of *Grit: The power of passion and perseverance*, points out that 'we get more self-controlled as we get older', connecting this in part to the maturation of the prefrontal cortex, and in part through exposure to strategies to build our self-control. The challenge, she highlights, is that for teenagers, the strength of their impulses is particularly strong.

Clearly at times teenagers are going to do things that aren't in their 'best interest'. That lack of self-control or discipline will also manifest in our classrooms. To help alleviate this, we need to try to set up positive role models in the classroom and secure peer norms that strive to bring out the best in teenagers.

Peer relationships

What mattered most to us as teenagers? I'm sure I'm not alone if I suggest that for me it was my friendship group and peers. For teenagers, how they are being perceived is a significant internal focus. There is a natural movement away from the authority figures and autonomy from parents – another means of asserting their growing independence. Those peer relationships can clearly be a positive or a negative thing.

Adolescents who spend significant time together are hugely influential in shaping each other's behaviours and attitudes. That pro-social element of the classroom is something we will reflect on later in the book. They are also at a greater level of sensitivity to feedback from their peers and others.

To return to Sarah-Jayne Blakemore (2018):

> 'The brain is particularly influenced by the environment during the teenage years and might be particularly amenable to learning certain skills. It's a sensitive period for social information, meaning that the brain is set up during adolescence to understand other people and to find out about other people's minds, their emotions. Brains at this time are good at understanding social hierarchies.'

That peer approval might not be sought from their friends. Harter (1990) has written extensively on this:

> 'Acknowledgement from peers in the public domain seems more critical than the personal regard of close friends, since close friends by definition provide support, and their positive feedback may not be perceived as necessarily self-enhancing. Thus, it would appear that the adolescent must turn to somewhat more objective sources of support – to the social mirror, as it were, in order to validate the self.'

We have seen that the teenage brain is lacking in its rationale functioning, which means that the hunger they feel for stimulation is not as constrained as it is in adults (although given how much time some of us spend on social media now, I'm not sure we do that effectively!). Anything in lessons that might be used to feed this hunger for stimulation (mobile phones, laptops, etc.) needs to be very carefully managed.

This is all compounded by the presence of the internet. I'm sure you will share some of the monumental mistakes I made as a teenager that I managed to quickly leave behind me. Mistakes teenagers make now can be very public and hard to step away from.

While new research into the teenage brain has been illuminating in generating a better understanding of them, so too has recent research about attachment styles.

ATTACHMENT STYLES

We all have an innate human desire for attachment: it is essential for forming positive relationships with others. This is at its most primal, however, when we are infants with no ability to look after our basic needs. At this integral point in human development, secure attachment helps to provide children with an emotional clarity that then plays a significant role in their future development. For decades, attachment has been a focus of substantial debate and research. In the 1950s, John Bowlby was the first of the attachment theorists and described it as 'lasting psychological connectedness between human beings'.

He believed that the relationships between children and their caregivers at the start of life have a demonstrable impact, influencing the rest of their lives. The first three years of a child's life are therefore integral in forming the ability to establish social, emotional and cognitive development and in establishing models for future relationships. Very simply, if the primary caregiver is available and responsive to a child's needs at the start of their life, the child develops security. They perceive their caregiver to be reliable and therefore do not fear the world.

The strange situation study

In the 1970s, Mary Ainsworth conducted the famous 'strange situation' study. The study observed children between the ages of 12 and 18 months, looking at how they responded to being left alone for a short period of time then reunited with their mothers. The results led her to identify three styles of attachment: secure attachment, ambivalent-insecure attachment, and avoidant-insecure attachment. Later, researchers Main and Solomon (1986) added a fourth attachment style called 'disorganised-insecure attachment' based on their own research.

A brief overview of these styles:

Ambivalent attachment: Children of this attachment style become very upset on the departure of their parent. Due to poor parental availability, these children cannot rely on their primary caregiver.

Avoidant attachment: These children reveal no clear preference between a caregiver and a stranger. This could be the result of either abuse or neglect, and these children will avoid seeking help throughout their lives.

Disorganised attachment: The behaviour of these children is less predictable, ranging from confusion to disorientation. For these children, their parents may be a source of both comfort and fear, resulting in a lack of predictability in their own behaviours.

Secure attachment: For these children there is distress when they are separated from caregivers and clear happiness when they return. This is the most common of attachment styles.

Colby Pearce, who has written extensively on attachment style, provides an overview in his book *A Short Introduction to Attachment and Attachment Disorder* of the impact caregivers' behaviour can have. He uses the acronym CARE: consistency, accessibility, responsiveness and emotional connectedness. All of these have a significant impact on the young person.

The research, however, is not limited to the 1960s and 1970s. The Attachment Research Community is a charity dedicated to supporting schools to develop attachment and trauma aware practice. They highlight on their website how the research into attachment theory has developed since the original work of Bowlby:

> 'Attachment theory and research has come a very long way since Bowlby's seminal papers from the 1960's and 70's. Since that time there have been advances in cutting-edge behavioral genetics, emotional neuroscience, quantitative psychology research and the effects of intergenerational trauma regarding the mechanisms and trajectories of attachment.' The Attachment Research Community (n. d.)

The impact

Writing for the *New York Times*, journalist and author Kate Murphy provocatively entitles her article 'Yes, it's your parents' fault', and highlights how attachment styles can profoundly influence how people behave in the future:

> 'By the end of our first year, we have stamped on our baby brains a pretty indelible template of how we think relationships work, based on how our parents or other primary caregivers treat us. From an evolutionary standpoint, this makes sense, because we need to figure out early on how to survive in our immediate environment.' (Murphy, 2017)

The implication is that attachment styles contribute to building an internal working model of young people's own identities and relationships. In their book *Attached*, psychiatrist Dr Amir Levine and psychologist Rachel Heller elaborate on how we often construct things based on our past experiences: 'It's kind of like searching in Google where it fills in based on what you searched before.'

For our purposes, we need to carefully reflect on how these attachment styles might manifest in the teenagers we work with. We should, of course, be aware that attachment styles are not the only contributing factor to behaviour in the classroom. As we shall see in the chapter on behaviour, there is a wide range of reasons why some teenagers may exhibit challenging behaviours, ranging from socio-economic factors to simple boredom.

In the focus of this chapter, however, how might children without secure attachments behave in the classroom?

The classroom

It is helpful to first consider what qualities adolescents with a secure attachment will be likely to demonstrate. The research implies that such students will have good self-esteem, they will be more open, self-reliant and independent, and they will be higher achievers. Their social skills overall are more likely to be developed, alongside their capacity to be resilient. The secure attachment style they have developed as a young child gives them a protective mask against anxiety and stress.

For those with an insecure attachment style, there is a chance that their behaviour will be less predictable and this can be mirrored in their experiences with relationships. They may engage in risky behaviours, present behavioural problems, and experience difficulties with emotional regulation, such as impulsivity.

Clearly, without that security in their own relationships, there is the likelihood that anxiety levels will be higher. Some young people may experience signs of post-traumatic stress disorder, and their capacity to self-soothe profound feelings of stress may be limited.

What can teachers do?

This chapter is not arguing that teachers should take on a surrogate therapist role or seek to diagnose young people with any kind of attachment style. This is one of the issues with attachment styles in education that David Didau and Nick Rose highlight in *What Every Teacher Needs to Know About Psychology*:

> 'Making judgements about the quality of attachment a student has with their parent isn't something teachers should be doing. Therefore, it's hard to see how a teacher's "diagnosis" of a student's attachment type could be remotely valid or applicable. Whether or not you might think a child has an insecure attachment really isn't a teacher's professional call.' (p. 232)

This is of course true – we are not qualified to make such judgements and it is neither morally nor ethically acceptable. The reality is that any precise information on the background of a young person should be provided by an educational psychologist or a child psychiatrist. If we do receive such guidance, it should be carefully reflected on and acted upon to provide the best environment for that young person.

However, in the same way that our capacity to work with teenagers is improved by our knowledge of the brain, our working relationships with teenagers can also be improved by our awareness of the research into attachment styles. This can at times explain – note, not excuse – some of the behaviours that teenagers will bring into our classrooms and how they might respond to our lessons. The basic awareness of different attachment styles will also help to solidify for us what kind of presence we should have in the classroom and the vital nature of how we speak to teenagers.

Parker and Levinson published a paper in 2018 – 'Student behaviour, motivation and the potential of attachment-aware schools to redefine the landscape' – and concluded 'that an approach to young people that acknowledged their identities and emotional needs was more likely to motivate them to make best use of educational opportunities' (Parker, 2018). This understanding of some of the emotional complexity of teenagers can help us to plan accordingly for the generic emotional climate and way of being in our classrooms. Professor Elizabeth Harlow, who has written extensively on attachment theory in schools, elaborates on this:

> 'The overarching aim of introducing attachment theory to the school environment, is to encourage a greater appreciation of the emotional needs of children and young people, which are understood in terms of relationship. The aim is for school staff members, and the school itself, to become a secure base, in order that the potential for children's learning and development is maximised.' (Harlow, 2018)

Later in this book we will explore communication strategies that will support teenagers who have not been the beneficiaries of a secure attachment style. The way we interact with teenagers is again given an added layer of significance: a consistent and calm approach will help them to feel safe. The clear demarcation of your role as a teacher is also important and boundaries play a significant role in that. We are, clearly, not the teenagers' primary caregivers, and that line should never be blurred.

In our section on behaviour, we will see how vital it is to depersonalise behavioural feedback and not to add fuel to either feelings of rejection or the inclination towards conflict that some adolescents may experience. Always communicating with warmth and positivity will help the young person feel safe in our company, as will having an environment that is structured and consistent.

Relationship building also becomes even more important. There can be a profound lack of trust between teenagers and adults, and forging a healthy connection with a teacher can be transformative. Making sure they feel safe and secure in our presence, and modelling compassionate and meaningful human relationships, is vital. To achieve that, we should be the kind of teachers that young people can check-in with and discuss how they are feeling. If that raises concerns, as with all forms of communication with young people in schools, we should report those concerns and not deal with them ourselves.

All of this does not negate the importance of having high expectations of what all teenagers can achieve. This balance of warmth and expectation is captured by Professor Elizabeth Harlow, who has written extensively on attachment theory in schools and has offered the following advice:

> 'A secure teacher-student relationship is characterised by trust and being attuned. The student would feel safe and able to seek help while the teacher would be able to console the student when required. Teachers should be educated in child development and have time to cultivate supportive relationships, but they also need to be authentic in their dealings, have high expectations of pupils, be well prepared for class, and facilitate pupil autonomy (in terms of being sensitive to the child's agenda and allowing some choice). If a child's biography has led to an insecure style of attachment, teachers may find them "hard to reach" and face challenges in building a trusting relationship. Nevertheless, efforts to build such a relationship can succeed.' (Harlow, 2018)

The complex psychological elements we have explored in this chapter bring us to the final message that is integral in our work with teenagers: to treat them with unconditional positive regard.

UNCONDITIONAL POSITIVE REGARD

This section of the book may seem dispiriting: how on earth do we now begin to find the tools to manage, let alone build, positive relationships with teenagers and inspire such a complex audience?

Part of what we need to demonstrate in our work with teenagers is what Carl Rogers defined in his therapeutic work in the 1950s as 'unconditional positive regard':

> 'To be with another in this [empathic] way means that for the time being, you lay aside your own views and values in order to enter another's world without prejudice. In some sense it means that you lay aside your self; this can only be done by persons who are secure enough in themselves that they know they will not get lost in what may turn out to be the strange or bizarre world of the other, and that they can comfortably return to their own world when they wish. Perhaps this description makes clear that being empathic is a complex, demanding, and strong—yet subtle and gentle—way of being.' (Rogers, 1980)

Our more defined understanding of just how complex the adolescent world is can help us embrace empathy.

Optimism

We have to strive to maintain an optimistic attitude and work hard to see the best in teenagers, not the worst. Our innate negativity bias makes this challenging, but it is vital if we want to project optimism and empathy in our classes.

It is perhaps a timely place to reiterate how utterly joyful working with young people can be and how the majority will present the very best version of themselves in the classroom (and save many of the more negative aspects of adolescence for their parents at home!). Focusing on that positive vision of teenagers, and pausing to recognise when they shine in our presence, will encourage us when a minority of them may present more challenges.

The reality is that the changes teenagers are going through make them fascinating and creative people to be around, and we see those changes manifest over the years we teach them. They are beginning to discover their purposes and to create new possibilities in our world. That, in all honesty, is not something that many adults hold on to – and working closely with them can help us to maintain that focus on optimism, growth and development. Dr Dan Siegel in his book *Brainstorm* highlights how important it is for us all to recognise that 'adolescence is not a stage to simply get over; it is a stage of life to cultivate well'.

Being seen

What teenagers are often looking for is a sense of understanding and feeling 'seen'. While we can't make excuses for teenagers and their behaviour, we can show that we know that they are experiencing major upheaval and recognise how difficult it can be for them. Dr John Coleman puts this particularly well:

> 'Young people take their development into their own hands. They make choices and select opinions all the time, and thus notions such as proactive coping, the development of competence, resilience and the building of connectedness are all central to our understanding of adolescence. Young people have skills, resources and enthusiasm to offer to the adult world. They are agents in their own development.' (Coleman, 2011)

Appreciating the depths of these autonomous agents – our teenage audience – is superfluous if we don't have the skill set to communicate effectively with them. We could be experts in the intricacies of the teenage brain development, but be unable to either inspire or control them on a wet Friday afternoon. This psychological background knowledge will help – but it needs to be balanced with the reality that teaching is a deeply practical and responsive communication process.

It is with the notion of performance that Friday afternoons demand that we will start. Our students, as we have seen, are at times not particularly enthused about being in our rooms in the first place. Time to capture them through the power of our presence.

We will start this exploration silently…

Part one summary: understand the complexity of the teenage audience

- Society often passes negative judgement on teenagers, which can have a clear impact on their self-esteem and cause a self-defeating cycle of poor behaviour.
- There are profound changes that occur in the teenage brain that influence how they behave in our classrooms, including their capacity to be rational, to manage their emotions and to be led by their peers.
- Alongside those changes are significant hormonal developments, which add to the insecurities of teenagers. Increased serotonin and dopamine in particular add to the teenage desire for rewards and fluctuations in stress levels.
- Recent research on attachment styles has opened up new insights into teenage behaviour, and an understanding of its complexity reinforces the importance of clarity and understanding in our classrooms.
- Part of our professional responsibility should be to think carefully about what influences teenage behaviour in the classroom.
- Our role in the classroom is to provide clarity, model patience, be compassionate and to hold teenagers with unconditional positive regard.

— PART TWO —

MASTER THE NON-VERBAL

'Nonverbal communication is an elaborate secret code that is written nowhere, known by none, and understood by all.'

Edward Sapir, *Language: An introduction to the study of speech*, 1949

TEEN TALK

How do you think a teacher should speak? What kind of body language should a good teacher use?

'A teacher should not make fun of a student for getting something really incorrect.'

'Friendly and open.'

'A good teacher should speak with a calm and more relaxed voice. They should be standing up and facing their students. They should be loud and clear.'

'Non-judgemental and open-minded to anything you have to say rather than acting like you're an idiot.'

'Positive attitude.'

'Teachers should endeavour to treat students like equals, using open body language and the vocabulary they would use if addressing another adult, explaining them only if requested to.'

'I like it when they're very passionate in their subject. The best teachers always love what they teach.'

'Be encouraging, but do not look over our shoulder. If we're struggling we will ask you for help, rather having the teacher check your every move.'

'Formal and friendly. It's a bit overbearing and strange if they are too "chummy" from the start. It's nice to be friends with your teacher but a bit odd if they act like your classmate from the beginning – it can also get confusing in how to communicate with your teacher, and what is rude to them or not.'

'Kindness.'

'They should be confident.'

'Be out there, funny, welcoming; some people say teachers shouldn't be your friends but I've had a close teacher-student relationship with the best teachers. Body language should be open.'

'Speak calmly and openly, with confident body language. I am more likely to listen to a teacher if I like and respect them. Aim to be kind and peaceful.'

'Any teacher worthy of the title should exude confidence and excitement in the way they display themselves so that the students can sense that positive energy and feel the same way.'

'A teacher should speak with compassion, with joy. Teachers should show respect to the people around them, both co-workers and pupils. I think, at the end of the day, teachers should show more than what they do. I've walked into schools and remembered nothing, but the most memorable teachers are the ones who make conversation, enjoy their time each day. Even just smiling does more than what anyone could ask for.'

'A teacher who is enthusiastic and genuinely loves their job is a great teacher because that enthusiasm sort of rubs off on you and you feel more desire to achieve. Just be kind and understand why people may act a certain way. Please don't raise your voice, it is really stressful and can cause anxiety attacks for me personally.'

'I personally do not have any problems with any teachers' speech or body language, but I know that it affects my friends. The most comfortable teachers to be around are those who just have that aura of relaxed confidence. A sense of humour also never hurts.'

'I don't think there's any one way a teacher should approach a classroom. There are many different personality types that respond differently to various types of teaching. Personally, I recognise I'm not super attentive to body language and I'm much more oriented towards actual words. With that being said, I think a good teacher would use body language and gestures to emphasise their point.'

'A teacher should be warm and use kind words with a student suffering through low self-esteem. Discourage openly showing favouritism. Include every student in discussions and listen to students.'

'A good teacher should respect the students and also listen to their feedback and modify lessons based on how everyone does in the subject. Teachers should also speak kindly.'

'Teachers, in my opinion, shouldn't be so uptight. I understand that they can't be fully casual with their students but having a teacher talk to me like they're writing an essay is just weird and I feel like I wouldn't enjoy their classes or be willing to confide in them for anything. Jokes are also really appreciated.'

'I think it should be very open. A conversation that engages students rather that a stiff strict lesson. Teachers need to make students care about what they are learning.'

'Depends on the age of the pupils. In the lower years they should be more authoritative and discipline more. However, as students get older, they should treat them with more maturity as they are older and let them do what they want more, e.g. don't tell them off as much.'

'A teacher should speak nicely, always offering help for students, and if someone doesn't understand the teacher shouldn't get all angry and throw a fit because someone hasn't understood. Teachers should take into consideration that some students are mentally ill and may need more help than the rest of the class.'

'A teacher who is enthusiastic and genuinely loves their job is a great teacher because that enthusiasm sort of rubs off on you and you feel more desire to achieve.'

'They should speak clearly, but they shouldn't get frustrated. If you shout at the student, it won't make the student change their behaviour, it will only make them more annoyed.'

'A teacher should talk to students in a friendly, respectful manner. They should always make eye contact and try to use simple language so that all students can engage and understand what is being spoken about in the lesson. This allows all students to feel involved and will boost the engagement and enjoyment of the lesson. Body language is key when teaching and the teacher should be using positive body language to encourage questions, discussion and debate in their lesson.'

A SILENT TEACHER PERFORMANCE: WHY BODY LANGUAGE MATTERS

It is time for a silent teacher performance. Let's say two teachers have agreed to be filmed for the purposes of this silent scrutiny, and we are the lucky recipients of their lessons. Our focus is on examining their non-verbal cues – for our purposes we shall define this as the act of communication without using words. We hit the mute button as we simultaneously watch the videos of these two teachers.

There is an eerie silence as we watch the split-screen performance in front of us. We can now see the sheer scale of the non-verbal decisions teachers make every day: what they do with their hands; how and where to stand; how to employ facial expressions; where to position themselves – the list is endless.

We can see now that everything we do is communication in the classroom.

Still and centred

On the left-hand side, the camera has zoomed in on a teacher at the front of the room. They are still and centred, with their hands moving slowly and emphatically enhancing their communication. Often those hands will rest together at the front of their bodies. Occasionally there is a more intentional gesture – one that seems to match their level of animation.

Their posture communicates authority: shoulders are open; their feet are spread evenly on the floor. Every so often, a warm smile pervades their face, they nod engagingly, and their facial expression is one of genuine encouragement and interest. There are moments in which they are leaning in and they are clearly attentive and listening intently to student responses. There are moments that feel like an eternity in which a pause is evident – they are waiting for attention to be focused on them in the room. There is another incident where we see the silent teacher 'stare': that menacing and skilled flash of a fierce facial expression that is directed towards an individual in the room. It lasts for three seconds at most, before a return to the easeful positivity.

A different world

Turning our attention to the other side of the split-screen, we see a different world. The teacher is sat in a hunched posture at the front of the desk. Although the video is still muted, we can sense a lack of energy, even a coldness emitting from their body language. The hands of this silent teacher remain limp at their side; their face is fixed in what appears to be a scowl. There is no notable change in persona as the young people enter the room. A PowerPoint presentation looms large at the front of the class.

This teacher's facial expression is fixed in its apathetic frustration for the entire duration of the lesson. They remain seated behind their computer screen as they start to speak to the class in front of them. Immediately it is clear there is conflict in the room, with the teacher seeming to exert more effort to raise the volume of their voice. Frustration and hostility radiates from them within minutes.

The teenage audience

As the cameras pan out to the teenage audience of both rooms, we also note a visible difference.

In our first classroom, it would be too much to suggest that every single young person is watching in attentive silence. What is clear, however, is the engagement and interest in their faces. A social norm has been established in this room: one that implies this teacher is someone who is not only listened to, but respected. There also appears to be genuine interest and warmth in some of their facial expressions and manner towards this teacher – a clear sense of a reciprocal relationship. Attention in the majority of cases, importantly, looks like it is channelled towards the teacher. The young people match the body language of the speaker; they are relatively still and appear to be listening.

In our second room, the young people's body language is emanating boredom and, in some cases, hostility. Their eyes show none of the eager enthusiasm that pervades the other classroom; rather it could be characterised by a sense of numbed acceptance: they have no choice but to be in this room. There are, of course, the young people who offer their attention and interest unreservedly – the teacher in front of them does not define their fate in any subject. More students in this room, however, are actively searching for distractions – their eyes scoping the room as they strive to attain the stimulation that their dopamine-sensitive minds are so desperate to secure.

Many of the teenage audience are as visibly slumped as the figure in front of them – or their hands are fiddling with pencils at best, mobile phones under the desk at worst.

Our silent classroom

We can now pause to envision our own silenced classrooms. We can detach ourselves in a zen-like fashion from our teaching at the front of the room and instead dispassionately watch ourselves from an outsider's vantage point. What do you see?

Communication happens on so many different micro-levels and, as this book will argue, simple changes in our practice can have a real impact on the quality of our teaching. An honest self-appraisal can help us to reflect on our current 'performance' levels and improve our communication. Let's begin this process by taking some time to reflect on the following 10 questions:

1. How conscious are you of your body language when you communicate with teenagers?
2. How well do you use hand gestures to convey messages in the classroom?
3. Do you use your posture to support you in communicating messages and building relationships in your classroom?
4. Do you control the tone and pitch of your voice?

5. Do you vary the volume of your voice to keep your students interested?

6. How do you use smiling in the classroom for effect?

7. Do you use effective eye contact? Do you have blind spots?

8. Are you conscious of non-verbal cues given by others in your classroom?

9. Do you reveal your emotions in your non-verbal behaviours?

10. How do you use personal space in the classroom?

These questions ask us to carefully reflect on how our non-verbal communication might appear to an observer. Do we send subliminal messages of passion and enthusiasm that convey our enjoyment of both the young people in front of us and our subject? Would we really want to be a teenager in our company for hours every week?

Our classroom non-verbal actions are often on auto-pilot; it is rarely something we do consciously. We don't have the time: we are on a conveyor belt of repetition with a new audience every hour who present a myriad of potential distractions. How can we be fully conscious of how we appear to them, or what we might be signalling to them?

The hidden dimension of communication

The truth is that our non-verbal communication betrays all kinds of emotions about us to young people. It is what the anthropologist Edward Hall calls 'the hidden dimension' of communication.

The adage that 90% of communication is non-verbal, which was first coined by Albert Mehrabian, a body-language researcher, was in fact introduced to highlight the comparison between verbal and non-verbal in demonstrating attitudes: 'When there are inconsistencies between attitudes communicated verbally and posturally, the postural component should dominate in determining the total attitude that is inferred' (Mehrabian, 1972).

As it isn't explicit, it may well be that we are not as skilful or attuned to this aspect of communication as we think – non-verbal communication, after all, can take on a variety of forms and have different impacts on different people. For example, if we are experiencing anxiety, while we might think we are shielding it from our students, in fact we can easily betray our true feelings by moving rapidly around the room. We also might think that we can mask our patent dislike of a young person (we have all been there!), but it might not be as hidden as we think. While our words might express something, our non-verbal cues could be entirely contradictory. Often our words are needed to clarify something we might have inadvertently revealed through our body language. The slight frown and slump in posture I demonstrate when my wife revealed mushroom pie was for dinner last night, for example, was much more revealing than my feigned verbal enthusiasm of 'great!'

Influential

What this chapter's contrasting anecdote illustrates is just how powerful our non-verbal communication is in terms of influencing the emotions and mood of the students in front of us. Young people, as they observe teachers throughout their school day, are privy to thousands of non-verbal cues, including postures, positioning, facial expressions, gestures, tone of voice and eye contact. All have a real impact on how they feel and learn.

The experience of education throughout the Covid-19 pandemic has made this exploration of non-verbal communication even more vital. The movement to online learning showed just how important our classroom spaces are for young people, with many experiencing a complete breakdown in learning communication. When teachers and pupils were then required to wear masks, communication was hampered even further. It taught us just how important facial expressions are in the classroom; how much a smile matters, and how much what we say can positively impact those in front of us. Trying to sustain some semblance of social distancing in the classroom also reinforced how body language and physicality are a vital part of learning.

This section of our communication toolkit will ask us to take the time to reflect on what happens underneath our words. We all want calm and purposeful classrooms, and taking the time to refine this area of our practice will add more than we think to this aim. Tiny changes to our practice in this area can help to drive forward our ability to communicate on all levels.

In this book we will unpick some of the most subtle and nuanced communication styles, recognising that something as simple as a smile can alter the mood of a classroom significantly. Let's start by considering where, and how, we position ourselves in the classroom.

POSITIONING

I know what you are thinking: positioning is hardly the most exciting place to begin an examination of how to secure presence and impact in our classrooms. It certainly isn't going to appear in the top 10 teacher CPD demands lists any time soon. But before you skip forward or reach for a distraction, let me reassure you: positioning in the classroom matters deeply. It is ultimately very simple: how can we position ourselves to maximise presence and impact?

Young people look to us for visual cues, and one of our core classroom aims is to get them to pay attention to us. Where we stand, sit or indeed crouch, will play a role in channelling that attention towards us. Positioning is also vital for relationships, and to encourage the enthusiasm and engagement we want from young people – it is an essential part of the communication toolkit.

If we consider the impact that social distancing had on positioning and personal space during the coronavirus pandemic, we see how much it matters in terms of fostering positive relationships and communication. The fact that we had to keep at least six feet from our loved ones and others made it very challenging to convey affection or communicate effectively. Those of us who taught while social distancing in the classroom will remember how challenging this was on so many different levels.

Traps

Where do we go wrong in our positioning in the classroom? One way is that we may appear too tentative in our physicality, lacking the bodily passion required to win over a classroom of teenagers. While that phrase felt rather odd to write, it becomes clearer why it is important when we consider the opposite to 'bodily passion': being wooden or frozen to the spot. As speakers, demonstrating any of those qualities would not endear us to any audience. In a classroom, they are the invitation to a riot.

Another frequent mistake is that we may draw an invisible line between ourselves and the students, which can inhibit building effective relationships with them. This includes hiding behind a computer screen or demonstrating reluctance to head towards the centre of the room. This physical inability to 'own our space' will be quickly picked up by teenagers – and they will start to take control of the classroom areas we are avoiding. There is also the issue of blind spots in the room. We might not be aware that there are pockets of the room in which young people know they cannot be seen, which they may use to their advantage.

So, what steps can we take to improve this aspect of our communication?

Know the room

If we are lucky enough to have a classroom, we need to develop an obsessive focus on how it works with our communication aims. That means we need to consider how our voice projects from each part of the classroom and where we can position ourselves to have the greatest impact. When I interviewed renowned public speaking coach, Cath Baxter, in preparation for this book, she highlighted this point – that any speaker must feel utterly in control of their environment in order to be effective.

We also need to reflect on potential blind spots – is there anywhere in the classroom where the young people in front of us can escape our razor-sharp focus? We should try to think beyond the most predictable areas. This should all come from our desire to engage and focus young people on what they need to learn and retain.

Whole-class instructions

We will unpick some phrases to secure this at a later point. For now, we are still imposing the mute button on the classroom.

There is real power in stillness at the front of the room for teachers. Finding a spot where we feel comfortable being static at the front of the room can give our whole-class instruction an air of predictability – we can always aim to use that particular area if that works for us. It shouldn't be too far forward or too far back, but at a central point that means we can take in the scope of the room. It also has to be an area where all students can see us and where behaviour management and checks for understanding can be undertaken effectively.

There is also value, however, in using the corners of the classroom strategically. In *Teach Like a Champion*, Doug Lemov (2010) explores what he calls 'Pastore's Perch' to position yourself effectively in the classroom. This is the place in the classroom where teachers can position themselves in order to see the whole room.

The importance of this is that students can see us watching the class and that they know that we are a teacher who is always scanning every angle of the room to ensure they are all focused.

Breaking the plane

The classroom itself can cause a shift in the power dynamic, and positioning plays a huge role in that. There is a need for a teacher to make it clear that they, not the students, own the space in the classroom. Part of the way to achieve that is through what Doug Lemov calls 'breaking the plane' – the plane being the imaginary line that runs the width of a classroom, between the front of the room and the place where your students are working.

This distinction is important, as it seems to present a psychological barrier in some classrooms. It is vital to building a rapport with our students and in helping to create a sense of a shared classroom mission – as soon as we have set students off and ensured they are focused, we should be diving in to work with them. This means that we are always on the move while students are working, and we are always taking in all of the students in the class. That might just be a friendly nod, a hand on a shoulder, or a quiet word of praise. It helps to create a classroom atmosphere that is both calm and accountable, and in which the teenagers are encouraged to monitor their own behaviour.

Proximity is important in this circulation – by standing close enough to students who might be distracted, we can silently address off-task behaviour. We can also be strategic in how we move around a room, focusing on the key areas that might not settle down immediately. It is very easy to aimlessly wander around a classroom, but in the most productive and calm classrooms, movement is calculated and organised.

Individual conversations

Moving around the room provides the perfect opportunity to strengthen both students' understanding and our relationships with them. Relationships in classrooms are arguably most often driven through content – that, after all, is what young people are looking to us for.

As we circulate a room, we can show genuine interest and curiosity in the work that young people are doing. We will unpick phrases for that at a later point, but our physicality is also important. We can use that moment to be level with the young person, matching eye contact and showing interest in both them and their work. These conversations are not the moment to show authoritative imposing; instead, we should be matching their body language and levels of interest. We also need to reflect on how much time we are spending with each individual student, and while this is an important area of differentiation, making sure that it isn't disproportionate is important.

While this positioning will be important in subliminally communicating both control of a classroom and a desire to build positive relationships, our facial expressions are also under our teenage audience's microscope. So, given that intense focus on our facial expressions, should we, or should we not, employ that most obvious sign of happiness human beings are capable of – a smile?

SMILING

'Don't smile until Christmas.' How many times as teachers have we heard that gloriously miserable phrase? How many of us were force-fed it in our first year of teaching and instead of employing a smile, ruled our classrooms with a dictatorship that gave no hint of the human beings under our frowns?

This advice has been consumed by generations of teachers, some of whom will sprint (miserably) past that Christmas benchmark and then just never ever smile at young people. These non-smiling teachers are working hard to offer their support to the depressingly small number of times the average adult smiles during the day: 11 (Knight, 2017).

Perception

How would we feel if we spent hours and hours every week in the same room with someone who never smiled? What would we think they thought about us, if they didn't display the most obvious and most universal sign of pleasure towards another person?

Let me be clear: in challenging the 'frown until Christmas' rationale, I'm not arguing for a clown caricature with endless smiling that serves only to unsettle young people. Smiling inanely at a class full of wild teenagers who are not paying a blind bit of attention to us will not be a particularly helpful behaviour-management strategy. I also know that as teachers we have to convey authority and assertiveness, and that clearly requires a professional persona. Being professional and smiling, however, are not a dichotomy: you can convey both control and assertiveness while allowing yourself to smile.

As with all classroom communication strategies, it is about balance.

Credibility

What does a smile show? A smile makes us more human – and that is surely something we want young people to see in us. An overly serious expression, in contrast, hints at an underlying insecurity, an earnestness, and an inability to relax. That kind of persona makes it hard for young people to feel a connection and warmth from us.

A smile gives us more credibility – we display that easy confidence and charisma that makes us look like we know what we are doing (even if the majority of the time we feel like we don't!). It gives young people a sense of security and helps them to feel like they can trust the person who is in front of them.

It all comes back to authenticity, as Roald Dahl writes about brilliantly here in *Danny, the Champion of the World*:

> 'I was glad my father was an eye-smiler. It meant he never gave me a fake smile because it's impossible to make your eyes twinkle if you aren't feeling twinkly yourself. A mouth-smile is different. You can fake a mouth-smile anytime you want, simply by moving your lips. I've also learned a real mouth-smile always has an eye-smile to go with it.'

Smiling also helps to diffuse conflict – and can be a brilliant way to throw a young person off guard. We appear more creative, more vibrant and brimming with passion.

Wellbeing

Do a furtive check around you now, just to make sure you don't appear like a complete lunatic. Now, try an unconstrained and effusive smile. Don't hold back – just hold it for as long as you can.

The first thing to notice is what happens to your brain. We manage to even trick ourselves when we smile. Darwin's facial-feedback hypothesis demonstrates that your brain recognises the movement of your facial muscles, which helps you to think positively about a situation. In the classroom context, this is important in helping to suffuse us with a sense of calm as we manage the classroom space.

These positive endorphins in the classroom are certainly needed: if we frown our way through every teaching day, we are going to end up feeling pretty miserable at the end of it. If we create classrooms in which smiling and, dare I say it, even laughter are encouraged, then everyone starts to feel more optimistic in that presence.

In the midst of a stressful lesson or day, a smile can be hugely rejuvenating. It can be a habit that can help us to take more pleasure in our working day and in the young people we are surrounded by.

Don't smile until Christmas? Nonsense.

EYE CONTACT

I consider myself a quiet and fairly shy person (interestingly sustained in the 20 years since I was a teenager!), so I am deeply conscious that eye contact is something that cannot be taken for granted. If I am speaking to someone new, or experiencing low self-confidence or high anxiety levels, I am aware that it is more challenging for me to maintain eye contact with others. If you read any books on confidence (I've desperately worked my way through a good few!), they will all espouse the value of maintaining and holding eye contact – and its correlation with both attentiveness and validation for others. And many of the eye contact platitudes do indeed ring true, particularly in the classroom setting.

The classroom

Eye contact in a classroom is important: it speaks of that confidence, of the ease and control that marks out the best teachers. Employing it sends a message to young people that you are aware of everything going on in your classroom. It increases the quality of the conversations that take place in your classroom.

In the one-on-one coaching work I have done with teachers, I was conscious of the need that we all have as individuals to feel like we are being genuinely listened to, and the role that eye contact and non-verbal affirmations can play in that. In the classroom, that desire to feel seen and recognised as an individual is equally, if not more, prominent than in communications with adults. Ultimately, eye contact helps in improving the perceptions that young people may have of their teacher, generating more feelings of trust and a sense of belonging in the classroom.

While it's important to be aware that eye contact is not easy for everyone we speak to, it can be easier to sustain when we have the teacher communication mask on. Interestingly, those of us with a predisposition to shyness can find that it slips when we are in performance flow with young people or talking about something we feel passionate about.

Starting a lesson

The start of a new lesson is a vital point for conveying positivity and maintaining relationships, and that can in part be achieved through eye contact. Standing at the door and greeting students as they enter a room sends a powerful message about how we feel about them. Welcoming every student with eye contact and a smile can make them feel reassured that they are entering a safe space – and that they are valued. The opposite approach – a teacher who is at their desk and doesn't acknowledge the young people who enter the room – is not likely to project positivity or excitement about the lesson ahead.

Greeting students as they enter allows us to pick up on any issues that our students may be experiencing, giving us a perfect opportunity to offer a quiet word of encouragement, or just to check in.

In a secondary school environment, many young people can easily drift through the day like a ghost. A soft 'is everything OK?' before a lesson begins can make a world of difference in helping young people feel seen and valued.

Whole-class instructions

We have already discussed the importance of managing attention in any classroom environment and the need for a teacher to channel this through their verbal and non-verbal communication. Purposeful eye contact can give power to our verbal communication, and help to ensure that young people will be taking in things we are saying.

Of course, as we all know too well (and as my wife will frequently remind me!) holding eye contact does not necessarily mean that we are taking in what is being said. While we should sensitively encourage young people to look at us while we talk, this needs to be balanced with the training in attention and listening that we will explore later in the book.

Making eye contact with young people on face value seems a simple and easy thing to fulfil. When faced with a room of 30 young people who might not be blessed with qualities of attentiveness themselves, it clearly becomes more challenging. I found myself failing miserably with this with a first year (Year 7) class recently. One student (we will call him Finlay) was starting to really dominate my attention. His interruptions and high energy levels meant that any instructions I was delivering at the front of the room seemed to be delivered entirely to him – giving him the attention he revelled in.

Being aware of this, I reflected on how I could spread this attentiveness across the class. The most obvious way was to encompass the spread of the entire room when communicating with the class. If we are referring to only a handful of students while we look round the room, we lack awareness of just how attentive the rest of the class is being. Managing to hold the attention of as many of the students in the room as possible improves the quality of listening that is taking place.

The cunningly named 'five-second swoop' can work well here. The aim is that five seconds should be spent on each section of the classroom when delivering instructions. If the room is split into three, that means we are spanning the room every 15 seconds and trying to hold the attention of a range of students within that section. By doing this, every student receives eye contact during a phase of longer whole-class instruction.

Circulation

There is a sort of joy in seeing a teacher crouched down with a young person, really engaging with them and providing them with assistance. It speaks so much more of shared endeavour and of compassion than a standing pose where a teacher speaks down on a teenager. That human level of communication is also appreciated and valued by the young person – even if they don't rush to offer such gushing feedback!

Here the eye contact is one-on-one, individual and personalised. It can again help to support whatever it is we are saying to them: a word of positivity or guidance on how to move forward with some aspect of their learning.

Respecting the disposition of the young person is also important here, so any one-on-one conversation requires us to take a softer tone of voice.

Managing behaviour

I'm sure that I am not the only teacher who has wistfully reflected on why I just can't master 'the look' – that innate talent some teachers have to silently communicate expectations through a swivel of the head and a piecing stare. It seems to be a part of some teachers' (or indeed, wives') DNA. In reality, the piercing look is something that can be practised and improved. Eye contact is central to it: we seek out the teenager who might be doing something they know they shouldn't and we maintain eye contact. Sometimes it might require a furrowing or a raise of an eyebrow, but more often, if we calmly hold their gaze, the illicit behaviour is instantly vaporised.

Building a rapport with teenagers is a crucial element of the secondary classroom. Focusing on eye contact can help us develop trusting and professional relationships with our students. But eye contact without physicality will only get us so far. Time to straighten up.

POSTURE

In October of 2021, I hurt my back. I would love to claim that this was heroically induced by some masculine sporting injury – perhaps through a desperate last-man rugby tackle – but it was, in fact, an injury I sustained when hoovering the stairs a little too vigorously. My students thought this particularly hilarious, and it clearly reinforced any 'teachers have no life' stereotypes they had previously associated me with (which are, of course, very much true in my respect).

Overnight I was reduced to a hobbling hunchback and found myself unable to stand up in front of my classes. It was very interesting to use this as an opportunity to take a bird's eye view of my teaching and to see how quickly this changed the dynamic of the classroom – and indeed my own levels of self-esteem and confidence.

And it led me to question: to what extent are our students influenced by our posture in the classroom? Does it impact their confidence in us? Does it alter how carefully they listen and respond to our teaching?

The power of body language

When Amy Cuddy delivered her TED talk in 2012 entitled 'Your body language may shape who you are', I doubt she thought that 10 years later it would have remarkably amassed over **66 million** views. That figure in itself, however, speaks volumes about how interested people are in shaping perception and the belief that posture can help to do this. In her book *Presence: Bringing Your Boldest Self to Your Biggest Challenges* she states, 'When our body language is confident and open, other people respond in kind, unconsciously reinforcing not only their perception of us but also our perception of ourselves.'

The title of her book – *Presence* – is interesting to pause on here; it is an essential part of managing a room of teenagers and in communicating effectively. So how can posture give us presence? To answer that, it may be useful here to consider some of the poor posture habits that teachers can fall into. After all, if we sit, stand or lie in a poor posture for sustained periods of time, it causes excessive strain on muscles, joints and ligaments. Teachers who stand every day for long periods of time will be very familiar with this!

The collapse

The experts at Harvard Medical School (2022) have come up with the rather non-scientific sounding 'collapsed' posture. As it sounds, this is when we are hunched forward in an exaggerated way (how I look right now, in fact, as I write this!). They argue that this is caused by modern habits such as working with computers and looking down at phones. For teachers, the downsides of this are significant: increased tension in our bodies causes straining in our voices and hampers the quality of our breathing. Another frequent complaint of teachers is tightness in the shoulders. Often this can be the result of tension in the body, as we may be raising our shoulders without realising.

How to stand

The first step is deceptively simple: try to keep your spine and body as straight as you possibly can. That should be balanced with relaxing your shoulders – so you don't hunch them – and squaring them towards your class. Swinging your arms every so often can help with this. As you stand, keep your weight balanced across both feet, and keep your feet parallel and hip width apart.

Try also to tilt your chin upwards. Thinking about appearing as tall as you can, and as open as you can, can be a helpful reminder. Another useful way to remind you to do this is to imagine a string pulling you gently up to the ceiling from the top of your head. Your hands, when not using the magnificent gestures we will explore in the next section, can either rest at your side or they can be 'nested' together with one hand within the other.

How do you know if you are achieving these lofty heights? It can be helpful to record yourself speaking – something you can do in your lessons or at home. This will give you a good insight into how you appear to an audience.

The benefits

Improving posture is useful for vocal projection, as it improves the quality of your breathing and allows you to project. Good posture is correlated with being in control and assertive in a room. It makes sense when you think about it: hunched shoulders and a collapsed posture give the impression of a lack of confidence, so the converse – a straight back and open shoulders – conveys confidence.

The Obama files

A man who exudes good posture, assertiveness and appeal is Barack Obama. However, if you take a quick look at a range of Obama's early speeches, he does not demonstrate the posture and body language he is now so widely respected for as a public speaker.

Good news then: it is a skill that can be practised, honed and developed. Luckily for us as teachers, we are presenting every single day. We have the capacity to pause to consider how we are talking to our audience and what we can do to improve. Being conscious of our physical presence as we communicate, setting some posture intentions and trying to stick to them will really help with the impact we can have.

That honing of body language is one that can prove instrumental in the management of classrooms. So, what do we do with these pesky hands?

HAND GESTURES

'Miss, how long can you go without using your hands when you talk?' My colleague had been set a challenge – her class had expressed their frustration at what they deemed her 'over-the-top' (their words, not mine) hand gestures. They wanted to see how long she could teach without them. She accepted the challenge, desperately tried to repress her expressive hand gestures and lasted approximately two minutes. Trying to communicate on any level without using hand gestures can be a significant challenge. An interesting illustration of this is to consider what you do when you are speaking on the phone. The reality is that most of us gesticulate fairly wildly even when on the phone – so there is little likelihood of us being able to curb it when teaching a subject we are passionate about in the classroom. Despite the fact that we have evolved over millions of years to use spoken language, our brains still want us to engage our hands to communicate.

However, we shouldn't aim to *not* use gestures. It would render us fairly emotionless – a kind of robot communicator. Gesturing is a vital component of language, adding meaningful and unique information to speech. Curbing gestures, therefore, is not the answer. We should strive to use them effectively to give power and authenticity to our communication.

The importance of hand gestures

A study by researchers from the University of Rome (Maricchiolo, Bonaiuto and Gnisci, 2005) gives four reasons why hand gestures are important:

1. **Hand gestures can help you describe what you're talking about**, both literally (e.g. when you talk about drawing a circle, you can

motion a circle with your hand) and metaphorically (e.g. you could motion a circle with your hand to say 'everybody').

2. **Hand gestures can help you point to people and things in your surroundings** (e.g. pointing at an object while you say 'look at that').

3. **Hand gestures can help you add emphasis and structure when you talk** (e.g. showing numbers when you count, '1, 2, 3...').

4. **Hand gestures give clues about your emotional state**.

Gestures, therefore, not only add power to an explanation, but they also help us to break down complex, abstract ideas and help our students retain information.

Energy and passion

For me, hand gestures are integral to creating energy and passion in the classroom. Without naming names, anyone we consider 'dull' is likely to manifest that monotony in their use of gestures. Speakers who put their hands in their pockets or behind their backs are often guilty of this – they are muting a vital part of effective communication. Without gestures we are rendered lifeless in communication. If there is a way for us to bring energy to a group of teenagers it should be ruthlessly employed!

Gestures add another dimension to what we are trying to convey and can be used to narrow the field of student attention. They function in tandem with speech, giving classroom communication an added richness and vitality. They can often, however, have downsides – overexuberant gestures can distract the teenagers in front of us. That appeared to be the rationale behind the class that attempted to ban my colleague from using her hands – they found it was diverting them from what they should really be paying attention to. There is, in fact, a technical term for this: 'verbal and non-verbal congruence'.

While to try to prescribe some sort of one-size-fits-all approach on how to use this valuable form of communication would be ludicrous, you should consider what you can do to use gestures to the best advantage in your classroom. For my colleague who was the recipient of the hand-gesture challenge, that would involve a transition from a sporadic, overly energetic use of hand gestures to using gestures with intent.

Our real question should be: how can we channel hand gestures for impact?

What to employ

We could take the rest of this book and microscopically analyse the different forms of hand gestures you can employ: the hand chop, the fist thrust, the fingertips grip, the finger point, the downward facing palm, the circulator, the upward facing palm, etc. I expect, however, that neither you nor I have the time, or indeed inclination, to go down this road. Instead, let's look at three golden rules.

1. Use gestures to break down cognitive load and aid retention.

Gestures can aid understanding and retention in the classroom. In doing so, we need to make our gestures explicit. As an English teacher, I find this can be a helpful way to elucidate the meaning of a word. Explaining the meaning of a 'circular narrative', to take a simple example, can brought to life by using a circular motion with both hands. Here, it is useful to draw students' attention to your hands, explaining that this is a deliberate gesture employed to help them understand and remember the information.

Explicit hand gestures can be applied across any subjects and can also help clarify any instructions you give, reducing the cognitive load for your students. For example, saying 'I would like you to work in groups of three' while holding up three fingers.

2. Use gestures to convey enthusiasm and passion

This comes back to the previous point about the manner in which we communicate non-verbally with teenagers. It is important to make sure that your hands are not lodged in your pockets, crossed in front of you or on your hips. Fiddling with your hair or scratching your face in the same place is never a good look either, serving only to either make you look nervous or to detract attention from what you are trying to teach. However, everyone has their own style when conveying enthusiasm and passion. Levels of interest and the dynamics of the room can be positively influenced by uninhibited gesturing. It can also play a role in boosting energy levels in a class.

Authenticity and trust – which we will explore later – rely on us conveying some sort of passion and emotion. They can both be built through our use of gestures – more movement conveys more passion. Always go for more animation rather than less – remember, communication is about persuasion and influence.

3. Use gestures to save energy

One of the intentions of this book is to try to save teachers' energy and to cut down on the wasted communications that can leave us emotionally drained at the end of a day. Developing a bespoke repertoire of hand signals that communicate precise messages can help to save some of that vital energy. Here are three very simple and easy-to-implement silent techniques:

1. **Thumbs up**. So easy, so positive. It can communicate praise and public recognition – it is a simple win–win situation.

2. **Finger to the lips**. A turn, a stare, and a finger to the lips can communicate displeasure with noise levels and help to encourage students to refocus.

3. **A pull of the ear**. Again, a simple strategy that will remind students of the importance of listening carefully.

Now that it's a thumbs up for hand gestures, do we need to think about what we wear?

APPEARANCE

'Sir, you're looking a bit rough!'

A quick glance in the mirror at break confirmed my worst fears: this delightful 14-year-old's fashion feedback was true. I was bleary eyed, my hair was even more out of control than usual, and my shirt looked like it had been ironed by a squirrel. To be fair to myself, my toddler and baby had clearly agreed an 'our parents shall not sleep tonight' pact the previous evening.

When reflecting on the quality of communication and how we can become more skilful in the classroom, however, this did give me pause for thought. Does the way we physically appear to the young people in front of us impact how they respond to us and their learning?

Balance

I realise I am on shaky ground here of sounding overly earnest at best and authoritarian at worst. I have worked in schools where dress codes for teachers have been manipulated. In my first leadership position in a school, I was 'instructed' to shave my head and wear a black suit. (Now, if that doesn't smack of obsessive controlling behaviour, I'm not sure what does.) Clearly that is going a step too far, and rest assured: I didn't last long in that role. I now refuse to wear a black suit and my hair (as the opening anecdote illustrates) is wildly uncontrolled.

Appearance in any form of public speaking, however, which requires us to present in a particular way, is helpful in adding another string to our communication bow.

Judgement

The notion of judging a book by its cover is a horrible cliché – but as with all clichés, it is grounded in common sense. The snap judgements that the cliché evokes are of course unfair, but in reality, we are all human and we all engage in them. Any communicator is 'judged', for want of a better word, before they start speaking, and a significant part of those preconceptions is on their appearance.

Teenagers are no more and no less guilty of using their innate biases to form instant judgements on people who stand in front of them. Like adults, teenagers will be assessing you on every level: age, professionality, potential for strictness vs friendliness, etc. How we appear, in reality, will contribute to each one of those snap judgements.

As a youthful 22-year-old working in my first role as a cover supervisor in the North East of England, I was forever being mistaken for one of the students – attempting to dress smartly seemed to be one of the only ways I could overcome that taunt. That is why, for me, the question of appearance is an important one to consider: it will influence how teenagers perceive us, so we should try to give ourselves an easy win.

Authenticity

There is, of course, a balance to be found. Authenticity is vital in teaching, and you need to feel comfortable in front of a class. Teaching in a onesie, however, obviously will not be appropriate, and there is a middle ground to be found.

For me as a male teacher this has always been ridiculously easy: a shirt and tie combination does the job just fine. I've always favoured a tie myself, just to keep up the sense of formality – and particularly to match what older male students will mostly be wearing in schools.

For the rest of us it helps to be as professional in our appearance as possible. In most schools we seem to spend an inordinate amount of time lecturing our students on various uniform issues. For that to not appear hopelessly hypocritical, we need to be in a position where they can't retort with some wise crack about how we look like we have been dragged through a bush backwards.

Individualism

That doesn't mean there isn't space for individualism – and the corporate approach to teacher appearance is stifling and controlling. Tattoos and dyed hair are all part and parcel of being an adult, and teachers should be no exception. If the dyed hair and tattoos are appropriate, teachers should not need to cover them. Teenagers shouldn't be presented with a homogenous entity of teachers, but rather see the delightful variation of human nature in their journeys through school!

If there is a mantra to remember, it would be that we don't want our appearance to detract from learning (as mine clearly did!), but instead for it to help project calm, composed authority.

TONE

'Don't use your teacher voice with me.'

Growing up with two parents as teachers (and indeed an extended family of teachers), I heard this phrase frequently. I'm sure it is ubiquitous in teacher homes across the globe: that accusation that we have become overly assertive in how we are communicating with our nearest and dearest. It is a phrase that also marks a transition in our exploration into 'silent' communication. Tone still comes under the umbrella of non-verbal communication, however, with its potential to modify or contradict the words you use.

Before we reflect on what we say, it is important to consider how we say it: how can we use that 'teacher voice' to achieve the greatest impact? Teenagers in our classrooms will invest time in 'reading' our voices – trying to discern through timing, pace, volume, tone and inflection what we are really trying to communicate. Undoubtedly there is a theatricality to the classroom. We are in a performance-based profession and a key aspect of that is to encourage listening in our audiences. The voice, in that respect, is a remarkably powerful tool. It is a tool, however, that can be our greatest ally or our greatest hindrance in the classroom.

Somehow, we need to find that challenging balance between being authoritative and appealing.

Contrasting voices

There are some voices that instantly attract attention: consider the gravitas of Barack Obama (in his later, deliberately practised years!) or the soothing tones of Sir David Attenborough. We incline our focus towards them – we want to hear more of what they have to say, and they can sustain our focus.

There are others, however, that achieve the opposite: they have voices that can range from being mildly irritating to having the potential to repel us completely. For those of us who belong to a certain generation, Janice in the sitcom *Friends* instantly springs to mind (that cackle and drawn-out phrase of 'oh my God' are unforgettable for all the wrong reasons!). There are, as harsh as it sounds, voices that we don't want to listen to.

No voice, of course, is perfect – but if we want teenagers to listen to our 'instrument' regularly, we need to consider how to use our vocal range effectively, and ultimately to make it as appealing as we can. Reflecting on how that voice might contribute to the management of classroom space is also important.

Traps

Walk through the corridors of any school and you are privy to a bombardment of contrasting 'teacher voices'. Let's consider each in turn.

1. One volume

It booms down the corridor, drowning out anything in its way. Without any change in volume or pitch whatsoever, this teacher voice doesn't do quiet. It evokes a range of responses in young people from fear to apathy. For the teacher, it can often lead to collapsing at the end of the school day, exhausted from sustaining such a high volume throughout the day.

2. Softly, softly

This is an interesting one: the teacher whose voice is soft and gentle. Some teenagers will thrive in this environment; it will be like a sea of calm that they feel utterly at home in. Some teenagers will, however, ruthlessly exploit the softer voice approach, making life for this teacher challenging.

3. The theatrical performer

The voice for this teacher is a fascinating and enjoyable tool, one that is never predictable. Their tone is employed to match their every mood: at times to convey their excitement in the learning process it is hugely energised – a breathless commitment to encouraging the same shared enthusiasm in their students. At other times it is sharp and assertive, using pitch to illustrate a sense of disappointment in the efforts or behaviour of the class.

4. The condescending

There is an interesting dynamic that often occurs in a classroom where a teacher seeks to match the language and tone of their students. This can be shrill, mocking and sarcastic, and is likely to prove unpopular with young people. It can often belittle teenagers and appear to treat them like small children.

Is there a definitive correct answer out of these options? No. There will be times when you use all these approaches. Like all aspects of classroom communication, however, this is a skill that can be developed.

What are the steps in doing so?

1. A self-audit

We may believe we are Michelle or Barack Obama incarnate – the epitome of a superb public speaker. Our own internal biases, however, are very likely to mean that we believe we are better than we actually are. When we record ourselves, however, there is literally no escape from our verbal flaws. When I first hosted the Tes English teaching podcast in 2018, I got a sharp insight into my many annoying verbal habits. A tendency to use elongated umms and to say 'kind of' or 'sort of' were the most criminal in a long list!

It is simple to achieve and you can do a recording on nearly any device now: a laptop, an iPad or most mobile phones. Once you have identified the voice aspects that you would like to work on, then you can seek to frequently reflect on the changes you have made. If your aim is to reduce the frequency in which you use certain words or fillers, replacing them with a pause can be very helpful, giving you the added bonus of slowing down your delivery.

2. Variation

When I interviewed voice coach and public speaking expert Cath Baxter in preparation for this section of the book, she placed much emphasis on variation as a means to engage and secure attention. She explored one technique with me that she called 'squeeze the juice'. The basic idea is that you vary the tone of your sentences by picking particular words that you are going to emphasise in more detail. For those particular words, you *squeeze the juice*; you give them more force and passion than you do with the rest of the words in the sentence. Another technique to accentuate variation is to finish each sentence strongly and vary your tone at the end of the sentence, making it clear when it is finished. This enables greater clarity and variation as you speak.

If you ever want an illustration of why this matters, and why voice is integral to public speaking, there is a fascinating video on YouTube called 'Margaret Thatcher voice before/after'. It shows her voice before working with a voice coach, just as she came to power, and then an interview with her after the voice coaching. The difference in her capacity to communicate with power is remarkable. What is also clear in the video is the difference in her breathing.

3. Breathing

Breath is hugely important in public speaking. The earlier chapter on posture will help to secure breathing that supports feeling calm and purposeful. One way that Cath Baxter argued that top performers deal with performance anxiety is to sigh with relief before they start any speaking engagement. That deep breath can quell lots of feelings of nervousness and leave you feeling ready to start talking.

This technique can also be applied during our verbal communication in the classroom. Often taking a deep breath while talking can allow for a pause and for students to catch up cognitively with what we are exploring. You should also try to leave space to breathe at the end of each sentence. If you do rush your communication and speak quickly, try to pause for breath at the end of each punctuation mark.

4. Pace

I am clearly a slow fan, having written a whole book on the value of slow teaching. When it comes to the pace at which we speak, the slow application is particularly important. Slowness gives us more authority and more clarity. It gives our (at times!) distracted teenagers the capacity to follow what we are saying. The pause becomes one of our greatest friends in the classroom in this respect, something we can employ with the breathing tips above. Holding that pause may feel unnatural at first, but we can see the impact in the way the audience begins to zoom in on us as we speak. Being conscious of the tone we are employing is also important in securing two of those elusive classroom qualities: authenticity and likeability.

AUTHENTICITY

In his online blog post, 'What I told my kids about doing well in college/university', Doug Lemov (2021) writes the following:

> 'There's one more pet theory I had in college that I've been reminded of and still believe in: Whenever possible choose classes based on the professor. A good teacher will make anything interesting.'

While I firmly agree with the sentiment, this statement led to a number of questions about teacher effectiveness and likeability. To what extent should a teacher be 'themselves' in the classroom? Which parts of themselves should they keep hidden, and which parts should they reveal? How important is authenticity in creating a teacher persona?

This is the last exploration of the non-verbal communication strategies: how can we generate an authentic persona? It matters because high up on student feedback about what makes teachers successful is authenticity, and for any positive relationships to be built it is a necessity. Doug Lemov's advice to his children rests on the chosen teacher being authentic. It is also more than just what we talk about, which we will move on to soon. It is also what we do in a classroom space that makes us authentic.

Persuasion

The notion of authenticity is often simply reduced to ideas of 'being yourself' or showing students that you 'care'. The reality is, however, that we all bring something entirely different from our own backgrounds. As Socrates states: 'To find yourself, think for yourself.' This temptation to act like a 'teacher' and adapt what you believe to be the most appropriate characteristics is often one of the biggest challenges teachers need to overcome. It is highlighted by Scrivener (2011):

'Be yourself. Don't feel that being a teacher means you have to behave like a "teacher". As far as possible, speak in ways you normally speak, respond as yourself rather than as you think a "teacher" should respond. Students ... very quickly see through someone who is role playing what they think a teacher should be. Authenticity in you tends to draw the best out of those you are working with.'

Clearly there is some truth in this: teenagers in particular will be very discerning in the classroom, having sat through many different versions of teacher personas. They can sense when a teacher is 'performing' and wooden. We also don't want to spend the majority of our working days behind some kind of ornate teacher 'mask' – that would be a recipe for resentment and frustration. We are all multifaceted and complex, and it is up to us which parts of those complex aspects we reveal in the classroom. You have to be comfortable in whatever teacher skin you reveal to the world.

There is also, however, the notion of professionalism, concerning what is appropriate or inappropriate in our interactions with teenagers. It could be argued that there is a fine balance and that having too much authenticity could tip into arrogance, resulting in negativity in the relationships we form with our students. We have all been in spaces where over-sharing has made us feel uncomfortable and ill at ease – something we would never want to encourage in the classroom.

What is authenticity?

What does it mean to be authentic? Carolin Kreber, a professor at the University of Edinburgh, has spent years wrestling with this concept. She makes the point that 'as long as authenticity remains only vaguely understood and ill defined ... it is ... not feasible to articulate a persuasive rationale for why we should be concerned with the phenomenon in the first place' (Kreber et al., 2007, p. 25).

In an attempt to define authenticity, they published a literature review and concluded with the following:

'The literature reviewed here revealed authenticity in teaching as an intriguing but also complex and multidimensional

> phenomenon. Authenticity in teaching involves features such as being genuine; becoming more self-aware; being defined by one's self rather than by others' expectations; bringing parts of oneself into interactions with students; and critically reflecting on self, others, relationships and context, and so forth. ... Authenticity is not just something that exclusively rests within myself ... for authenticity to be meaningful it needs to be sought in relation to issues that matter crucially' (ibid, pp. 40–41).

Let's examine some of these areas in more detail.

Genuine

What contributes to a teacher coming across as genuine? A number of points that have been raised so far in this book are applicable here: that sense of physicality matters – our proximity to students, as well as our enthusiasm in the way we communicate non-verbally. As we have already identified, the simple process of smiling and showing warmth also helps to create a sense of trust. Bringing some aspect of our personality and humour into interactions with teenagers also matters in creating an authentic persona.

Also, as Shakespeare wrote, 'no legacy is so rich as honesty'. This can be powerful for our teenage audience, particularly when it is appropriate honesty about mistakes we have made or honesty about what we have struggled with in our own learning. Our honesty helps teenagers to see us as humans with our own complex learning histories. At times, that can be difficult for teenagers to perceive – we are often just another expert adult learner, who they struggle to empathise with or see as having similar experiences. We should encourage openness and the capacity to acknowledge mistakes in their own behaviour in the classroom – so modelling it will help them to see this as acceptable.

In that respect, there is an element of vulnerability to being an effective teacher – a balance between keeping things back and revealing some of ourselves to the teenagers in front of us. When we are really passionate about teaching, we bring that natural energy that makes us appear more authentic and genuine.

Self-aware

It is difficult to appear authentic in a classroom unless we are deeply self-aware. This can be more challenging when you are at the start of your career and coming back to a school setting after university and teacher training. Having some sense of our complex identity will help us to manifest authenticity in the classroom. That can be values based: what matters to us, what kind of person we aspire to be, and what is at the heart of successful communication for us? It can also be more strengths based: what are our strengths and what do we perceive our weaknesses to be?

When it comes to reflecting on our capacity to manage behaviour in the secondary classroom, self-awareness in regard to managing our emotions is also vital. Are we aware of what our anger trigger points are? Do we have the capacity to calm ourselves when faced with provocation and tension?

Now we have reflected and started to hone the performance aspects of our teaching, we can start to move more deeply into a world that requires endless patience and self-regulation: behaviour management. We start here because if we don't get this aspect of our classroom practice right, then the reality is that everything else crumbles around us. Our lessons may be packed full of brilliant explanations, fantastic questions and clear learning, but if we don't have the conditions to enable that learning, nothing happens.

Hold on tight. Some of our teenagers can make this particular communication aspect of classroom life challenging.

Part two summary: master the non-verbal

- Our non-verbal communication in the classroom is vital – we are under an intense microscope from teenagers, and all communication matters.
- Any effective communicator demonstrates ownership over their 'space'. We need to position ourselves so that we are portraying our confidence in a classroom.
- Two simple areas can help us to build positive relationships and make teenagers feel included: smiling and sustaining eye contact throughout the room.

- Posture and appearance can help in maintaining a calm and confident persona, and also prevent the array of aches that seem to be part of being a classroom teacher!
- There is a delicate balance with hand gestures – using them with intent to support both enthusiasm and messaging can help increase understanding and retention.
- Given how much we talk, the tone we use can be instrumental in securing attention and building an atmosphere fit for learning. Variation will help to ensure impact.
- Finding authenticity in our classroom persona is important, particularly in our work with older students: self-awareness, reflection and appropriate honesty will help us to come across as genuine in the eyes of teenagers.

PART THREE

SCRIPT AND TEACH BEHAVIOUR

'Human behaviour flows from three main sources: desire, emotion and knowledge.'

Plato

TEEN TALK

What can a teacher say and do that will improve behaviour in a classroom?

'Do a reward system to encourage students to do better.'

'Help everyone and make sure that you don't just help certain people.'

'Reward students for good behaviour, even if it's like one free period every few weeks.'

'Behaviour in a classroom is best when there is a good balance between working and joking around and this balance is understood by everyone present.'

'Set out expectations from the beginning. Use sanctions when sanctions apply.'

'Overall, I notice once students decide that a teacher is bad, they don't change that opinion. So really, a teacher should provide a good example of teaching at the start of the year and continue that way, by creating (or at least the subject could) good fun lessons, with a mix of different elements. Not too much talking, discipline, etc.'

'They could be upbeat and not be shy.'

'Give us a reward as a class if we all do well on something.'

'Be firm, not strict. Too lenient and students will stop paying attention and think it is OK to not listen/be rude, but too strict and people will be unwilling to listen or communicate with the teacher which will affect their attitude in the class and towards the subject. Communication with students and being perceived as friendly will improve behaviour.'

'Fun activities and positive energy would help improve behaviour in the classroom.'

'The idea of "shouting" is not beneficial to pupils, unless they are a bunch of kids who don't want to get into trouble (which, in a school setting, is nearly impossible). I think teachers need to put what they say in use, or "practice what they preach". At the end of it, teachers need to establish a set of rules that kids should be reminded of, and try to figure out what is going on. Kids on the top of the behaviour list may have just as much going on as kids at the bottom. They all need to be checked on.'

'A good teacher needs to like the subject they are teaching, and the students need to feel like they're being seen and heard, but that doesn't mean being too lenient. Some of my favourite teachers are strict.'

'I recognise it's an extremely difficult situation – managing a room full of teenagers is probably one of the hardest things anyone could do. Like I said earlier, people react in different ways. I think that being a more fun, relaxed, and caring teacher in general would improve classroom behaviour. For me, knowing that a teacher is approachable obviously makes them more human. If I see a teacher as an authority figure who's really just there to install a bunch of rules and give a boring lecture while essentially ignoring me, it makes it a lot easier for me to justify breaking those rules. Obviously, though, there's a time to be strict, even while being the "fun" teacher. If students think that a teacher won't care if they break the rules, there are definitely some that'll test the limits.'

'Be calm with everyone and not get angry.'

'Repeat the rules; remind people.'

'Honestly, I don't know. Teachers being strict isn't the answer, though I'm a student so I'm biased, but it really lowers moral and makes me dislike the class. I feel like for all my classes the teachers didn't do anything to make the classes better. The classes just got better from people dropping the classes they don't like and wanting to learn in the classes they do like. Compare an uninterested S1 class to an S6 class that need and enjoy the subject. The S6 class are obviously going to be less rowdy and misbehave less.'

'Positive relationships between student and teacher with clear boundaries. Treat them like people and find a way to show that you care.'

'They could have warnings and then if warnings are reached then they talk to the disruptive pupil after class privately. They should also listen to the pupil's viewpoint and consider that there are most likely outlying factors that are causing the issue which they should try to address. If behaviour continues, try to give more attention to the pupil and check that they know what to do as they may be struggling, and are therefore being distracting as they don't know what else to do.'

'A teacher should only raise their voice when there is a valid reason to. The teacher could try having some sort of "game day" where every Friday the students can relax and play some board games, or games that have something to do with the lesson, which would make students more comfortable in the class and more excited to join, and may improve any bad behaviour since the teacher could cancel the game day if there is any bad behaviour.'

'I think it's important to build relationships with pupils in the classroom and to reach a mutual understanding with young people that you are here for them, you genuinely care and that you are here to help. A clear understanding of boundaries and "expectations" (not to be confused with pressures) from the beginning is important. However, it should be approached in a friendly manner, as opposed to a lecture.'

'Having just finished high school, I can say that I do not believe in shouting at pupils, in handing out detentions or in ridiculing pupils in front of other young people. I believe positive reinforcements are important. I believe that each young person (under the right circumstances) has the potential to achieve so much, and so I feel in a classroom, the best way to manage behaviour is to work to remove barriers and create an environment where young people can reach this potential. I believe that when a young person does "act out" it's not necessarily a behavioural issue, but more deep-rooted in experience and personal problems.'

'I feel that a trauma-informed lens in education is massively important, and combined with this should be person-centred care. While I acknowledge it is incredibly difficult to manage a classroom and the behaviour of young people at times, it's important to remain calm and not to jump to punishment, but to actually help the young person and the root of the problem.'

WHY BEHAVIOUR MATTERS

Behaviour has the capacity to utterly destroy teachers and careers in education. It has the ability to make us question why we entered the profession, and when faced with unrelentingly bad behaviour, it ultimately can cause some to leave it completely. In a secondary context, behaviour can be particularly demoralising. Yes, each lesson represents a new start and a new opportunity, but if that equates to six or seven lessons a day with recurring incidents of challenging behaviour, our resilience levels are brutally tested.

In the context of the aim of this book – to cultivate skilful classroom communication – it is very challenging to maintain a calm and consistent style in the face of repeated bad behaviour. It also has the capacity to destroy learning. If behaviour is not managed – and make no mistake, in the secondary context, it needs to be managed – then there will be a hugely detrimental impact on learning.

Behavioural norms

Some teenagers have an amazing ability to learn regardless of the conditions – they have a filter that somehow manages to shut out the distractions and they can focus on their work. A number, however, will follow behavioural norms that are set in a classroom – for good or for bad. And those behavioural norms, once established, are difficult to recover from. Just how often have we heard teenagers indelibly define a teacher as 'not being able to control us' or as being 'too soft/laid back'? How often have we heard, arguably the most damning encapsulation of them all, 'we don't do anything in their lesson'?

We have seen already in this book that peer validation and rewards are very important for teenagers. Our first battle, therefore, is to make it clear that in our lessons there are very clear behavioural norms that teenagers must follow.

What do we want to communicate in terms of behaviour?

The short answer is everything. All aspects of behaviour need to be *taught*, modelled and repetitively conveyed. We want to make explicit, calmly and patiently, our levels of expectations. We want learning to be the focus and to convey an utter sense of horror when learning is not given the attention that we want it to have in *our* classroom. Eventually, through this patient and repetitive teaching of behaviour, we want an atmosphere of respect. That respect involves individuals taking ownership of their behaviour and regulating how they manage themselves in our classroom space.

We want to encourage the teenagers in our classes to be self-reflective, to have the capacity to recognise when they are demonstrating less desirable behaviours and to subsequently make changes in how they are behaving. A recent report from the Education Endowment Foundation had this philosophy at its core:

> 'Pupils who are aware of their own behaviour, who can self-regulate and deploy coping skills, will be less likely to misbehave in school. Once such strategies have been developed and strengthened, they turn into essential life skills and help students to become motivated and determined to succeed. Behaviour-for-learning approaches can be supported by the evidence on social and emotional learning, self-regulation, and essential life skills.' (EEF, 2021)

I also firmly believe we need to communicate ownership. Yes, we need to follow school policies and seek support from others, but we also need to show young people that we ultimately are in control of our classroom space. That involves using support networks and policies, but also demonstrating that we will not rely on others to tackle or manage poor behaviour.

The behavioural expert

It all sounds very simple, but watch any 'expert' teacher at work and you will see a wide and complex array of communication strategies that appear to be seamlessly employed. They don't demand compliance from young people; they model it, encourage it, and grow it. They are always, without exception, the adult in the room. They don't demean themselves or the young people around them. They don't roar in rage and inspire an atmosphere of fear – they just somehow, magically, manage the room.

Like most things in life worth learning, our job is to watch, listen, steal and then practise. It is also our job to invest time in talking to behaviour experts in order to understand what they have spent hours mastering before we arrived in such a well-managed space. Those experts haven't achieved optimal behaviour in their classroom overnight; they have made many, many mistakes in the management of behaviour.

Writing this section of the book has been one of the easiest. I don't say that out of arrogance. I have had to work exceptionally hard at managing behaviour in classrooms. I have had to learn this craft painfully, mistake after mistake. Hours of reading and carefully observing have improved my management of behaviour – but I am very far from being one of the experts I describe above.

My natural manner is to be positive and very enthusiastic in the classroom – a full-on presence that tries to dominate the classroom in part through the force of personality (and through channelling anxiety into delivery!). The fact that this is the very antithesis of my 'normal' personality means this can be draining, but it has overall led to most young people in general responding positively.

Learning from mistakes

I have always taught in fairly tough comprehensive secondary environments however, and there have been some classes that haven't responded to my positive, enthusiastic approach. (There is one example that is always at the back of my mind: a very challenging Year 9 class in my first year at a coastal school that had just been put into the Ofsted category of special measures.) What I have learned in this painstakingly thorough (and often desperate) attempt to improve behaviour in my classroom is that much of effective behavioural management is highly scripted and finely tuned through hours of reflecting on how teenagers might respond to things.

We now need to apply that scripted level of detail to every aspect of our lessons. Let's start by seeking to understand some of the behaviours teenagers will inevitably present.

WHY DO (SOME) TEENAGERS MISBEHAVE?

There has been a common thread running through this book already: the vital importance of seeking understanding and compassion for teenagers. It is clear that doing so will make us more patient and aware in our classrooms. Behaviour in classrooms is influenced, as we have already seen, by a huge range of issues, and having an awareness of context will help us to make choices about how to respond effectively.

Patient dispassion becomes more challenging when we are faced with the emotional reality of difficult behaviour in our classrooms. Let's take ourselves out of the heat of the emotional firecracker of the classroom and consider this objectively: why are some teenagers quick to demonstrate negative behaviours?

For the purposes of this section, we are looking at teenagers as a homogenous group. There will, however, be a wide range of other complex needs that some teenagers may have that will clearly impact how they behave in our lessons. Our earlier exploration of the teenage brain, attachment styles and the impact of trauma have begun to highlight this. It is also important to remember that this level of understanding for why some young people choose to misbehave (which, of course, can never be complete) does not mean we excuse it or justify it. Instead, we are empowered by our knowledge, and we should recognise that it supports our aims to achieve the best for them.

By being very clear in our behavioural communication and relentless in high behavioural expectations in our lessons, we are making sure that these teenagers have the best possible opportunity to make the choices they need to succeed.

Social approval

We have talked already about the social justification that teenagers seek, but it is worth reiterating it here. Remember that in childhood the only approval that young children really seek is from their parents and perhaps their siblings. That becomes much more complex in adolescence, when the approval of friends is a significant influence in how they behave. To return to Sarah-Jayne Blakemore in *Inventing Ourselves: The Secret Life of the Teenage Brain*:

> 'The development of the social brain during adolescence suggests that during this period of life the brain is particularly susceptible to social pressure, but also to the social experiences that adolescents have around them, and the social opportunities that are given to them.'

The classroom, of course, is the perfect place to find approval and display some of these impulsive behaviours. Teenage approval, unfortunately, is often not correlated with working industrially or throwing your hand up for every answer. Instead, it is often gained through mucking around. Part of our job in this section of the book is to provide a language script that can seek to battle against these peer dynamics and instead signal the importance of self-control and achievement.

Challenging home environments

Behaviour itself is sometimes a form of communication – but not always. Some teenagers have home environments that can be very challenging. The way in which their behaviours are managed may be hugely confrontational, and in some cases there may be no boundaries or guidance on how to behave. This can often result in a patent distrust of authority figures or anyone who tries to impose certain ways of acting. It can foster resentment in the classroom – we have all been subject to ornate eye-rolls and sighing when we attempt to impose rules or behaviours on a teenager.

That is why we have to be so conscious of our position as role models in the classroom and how respect needs to permeate our interactions with teenagers. While they might not always respond respectfully themselves, we should never seem to belittle or humiliate teenagers.

We will also never be privy to all that happens to a teenager outside our classrooms, or indeed how certain situations manifest for that young person. Being conscious of this, and trying to maintain an open and forgiving mindset that depersonalises behaviour, is vital in sustaining good relationships. Checking in with young people and being prepared to genuinely listen can be incredibly helpful for them.

Lack of understanding

We have clarified that thinking is a very challenging thing to do and that we will often seek distraction to deviate from having to think deeply. When a task we have set hasn't given teenagers an opportunity to be successful, or we haven't made clear what is expected of them, there is much more potential for behaviour to slide. Part four (LEAP in classroom discussion) will focus on how we can use our communication skills to prevent this occurring in our classrooms.

Boredom

Sometimes the rationale for poor behaviour is much simpler: our students are simply bored and do not want to be in a classroom with us. The outside world with its instant gratifications is clearly much more interesting. The artificial nature of the classroom setting – being forced into a room to learn something students may have no intrinsic interest in – can provide some justification for this form of behaviour. We will explore ways of dealing with this throughout this section. One thing we should avoid, however, is falling into the trap of believing that we need to constantly entertain teenagers. We are there to educate, not entertain.

Through making the content of our subject meaningful for them and showing them how it can benefit their lives, we begin to challenge some of that boredom. A theme running through this book is that in the secondary context, relationships are often built through the passion we have for our subjects – making subjects 'sing' to them and showing how we can foster teenagers' confidence in them. That focus on subject knowledge, however, also needs to be balanced with maintaining a sense of humour!

There will be a range of other reasons why some teenagers will be disruptive in the classroom. We are all complex and multifaceted. Being proactive and making sure that we can actively plan to manage disruption and promote good behaviour will now be our focus. Our first step is to forensically examine what needs to happen before our teenage customers even enter the classroom. What will help us to present a calm and assertive manner when they do eventually arrive?

PRE-LESSON

This section aims to reinforce the points about non-verbal and body language that have come before, with a specific lens on managing behaviour. Much of the effective management of teenage behaviour is an act. By default, it is an entirely unnatural situation: you are in a room with up to 30 teenagers and you need to communicate that you are in charge. To make that explicit: 1:30 is our ratio. The teenagers themselves are aware of this power dynamic, a contributor to the 'Teen Talks' in the opening of this chapter calls it 'one of the hardest things anyone can do'.

With that kind of ratio, you need to be very clear on what your success plan is for behaviour.

It is leadership at its most brutal (which is why I would be tempted to argue with any effective teacher who says they don't have leadership qualities), assertiveness at its most primitive and a true test of the force of our acting. Note I haven't used 'personality': instead, it is about our capacity to act out a range of behaviours.

Communication in this context is instant: as soon as teenagers enter a room, behavioural norms are established, and they will be watching each other carefully to assess the parameters of what they can and cannot do. Establishing instant expectations and an aura of confidence and control is an immediate priority.

So how do we do it?

Seating plan

While our focus is on communication inside the classroom, it would be a mistake to not examine practical steps we can take to ease that communication once a lesson begins. The first step is simple: have a seating plan.

Teenagers will, quite naturally, instantly revolt against the mere notion of a seating plan. They will argue passionately (and often very persuasively) that if they are sat next to their best friend Esmerelda, they will be more efficient than Steve Jobs on a good day. Your very sensible counter that they aren't likely to concentrate if they are indeed sat next to Esmerelda, will be ruthlessly ignored – and will waste valuable learning time.

While this may seem rather harsh on our teenage customers, our investigation into their rapidly forming brains justified that most of the time what they believe is best for them is ultimately not. If you let a class sit where they want, you will find that even the best, most well-mannered students change when they are sat beside their chums. Again, it comes down to the ease of the distraction – being beside their friends makes it far too easy for them to give in to distraction. Would we listen to someone talk (often about something we have very little intrinsic interest in), if we were sat next to our best friends?

Instead of entering into any dialogue about where students sit, we need a very firm and clear rejoinder: 'In my lessons there is always a seating plan. I decide where you sit in my classroom.' On paper that sounds a bit harsh, but there really is not much you can argue with here. The pronoun use is vital in conveying an assertive tone and a sense of ownership over the classroom: 'I' once and 'my' twice. This doesn't have to be uttered in a draconian growl with spit flying from the side of our mouths in exaggerated rage. It can be clear and respectful, and followed by something positive: 'I'm really looking forward to starting our lesson, so sit down, thank you.'

Making sure that we are confident in our knowledge of our students is also important. The more empowered we are about what is impacting their behaviour in the classroom, the easier it will be to tailor our strategies to support them to be the best version of themselves.

Names

It is a very simple statement, but a 'names-rich' classroom has better behaviour management. In fact, one of the most essential of all the communication classroom strategies in this book is to know and use the teenagers' names regularly. Doing so helps them to believe they are valued, appreciated and understood. The seating plan is a secret weapon in this regard because in the first few lessons you can scan it for reminders. It makes the management of both relationships and behaviour much easier.

Planning

Our capacity to manage a space will become easier if we plan for how that lesson – be it 50 minutes, an hour or longer – is going to proceed. If we are very clear on the content, the expectations and what we want the outcome to be, then there is a much greater likelihood that our lesson will be one that speaks of confidence and clarity. When planning, we must carefully consider how we are going to manage transitions and how the attention of the young people is managed throughout. If the attention isn't managed, then we risk handing them the opportunity to procrastinate or misbehave. It is helpful to reflect on what students will be thinking about as we plan lessons.

That behavioural planning takes some thinking beforehand and some pessimistic visualisation. That means reflecting on a worst-case scenario, not to inspire a fear so great we find ourselves hidden in the nearest cupboard, but to make sure we have planned out how we can minimise the potential for misbehaviour.

Keeping opportunity for 'drift' to a minimum is a good starting point for this. Any time that isn't accounted for or any activity that is not appropriately structured and 'free' (think unstructured group work without any real outcome) means that there is more likelihood of negative behaviours occurring. This is challenging at the start of a teaching career when that ability to foresee potential pitfalls in a lesson is not quite attuned. If this applies to you, asking a more experienced colleague to look over a lesson plan can be a very helpful process. It allows you to articulate what you are expecting and will no doubt lead to some revelations that might have passed you by.

Have resources ready

The less time we spend running around flapping bits of paper and handing things out in a lesson, the better. It is challenging to maintain a front of control (or in fact to do anything) if you are having to multitask significantly. Although it is a skill we need to possess in our lessons, the more we minimise it, the more we look in charge. Our planning should take this into account: how are things being distributed around the room? It might be that you have some of the students do this or have things already on desks before students enter the room, but either way, the simpler it is and the more routine it is, the better.

Know the systems inside out

Your behavioural communication is often dictated by school policies. You might disagree with those policies or feel that they aren't what you want to do in your classroom, but not using them will inevitably cause problems. Renegade teachers are unfortunately not action heroes like Bruce Willis in *Die Hard*; instead they ultimately confuse young people and end up confused themselves about what they are trying to achieve in their classrooms.

Know your non-negotiables

Finding ways to be consistent are also remarkably important, so that Sharron receives the same behavioural focus as Jimmy. Teenagers will always argue that you are being 'unfair' or 'picking on them', so making sure there is no evidence to support such statements is always very important. How many warnings should young people get? When are they moved seats? Having utter clarity on these systems, and knowing the language you should use to communicate them, is vital.

This journey through communication in the classroom has returned to the word 'clarity' over and over again. Making sure that we are absolutely clear on what our behavioural non-negotiables are is an essential process. They may well be dictated by the school, but going through this thinking before a lesson starts means you are very well prepared.

Get in the zone

An excellent teacher I worked with at a tough school in my training year told me that managing behaviour was often 'a war of attrition'. In those early days of idealisation, I felt I could connect emotionally with every teenager and win them over through my passion for English as a subject. Unsurprisingly, that failed pretty miserably.

That teacher reassured me that these failed attempts were not a personal reflection on me, but rather the innate resistance that some teenagers have to both authority and education. But that was balanced with clear feedback: while it wasn't my fault, it was my responsibility as the classroom teacher to take ownership over managing that behaviour. He continued that I was being too 'nice'. Instead, he felt I needed to channel a steely assertiveness that balanced that pleasant and dignified way of communicating with young people with a clear conviction that I wasn't to be messed with.

That requires a certain kind of mental preparation – an almost gladiatorial 'getting in the zone'. Unless you are a remarkably assertive person (which I am very, very much not), then going through this process will help make sure you are ready to approach whatever challenges the lesson might throw your way.

Anxiety

There is, of course, anxiety associated with behaviour. As we await a lesson in which we know we are going to be presented with 'challenging' students, it can be very easy to fixate on those uncomfortable feelings of anxiety. That might be that horrible feeling in your stomach that is associated with anxiety.

Consultant Peter Koestenbaum (2000) writes about an excellent way of reframing such thinking, based on work by Peter Block:

> 'Anxiety, far from being a sickness, is the actual experience of being strong, of growing, of building character, of achieving pride. … Anxiety … *is how it feels to grow authentically into the human being we were meant to be.*'

In growing as a teacher, we have to learn to adapt to these inevitable feelings of anxiety and frustration. Part of achieving that is by recognising and valuing the emotions we feel, and channelling them into something positive that can give us energy to get the best out of classes.

Popularity

It is also about understanding that teaching is not a popularity contest – and you must be prepared to be disliked by the students you teach. That can be challenging, particularly for those of us who might veer towards people pleasing. It is vital to remember, however, that there is so much time to build positive relationships with young people, and the various ways that those relationships can be built are complex.

Particularly at the start of a school year, that notion of being 'liked' should be at the back of our minds: instead, we need to be obsessing over clarity and consistency. Michael Marland sums this up in his teaching classic *The Craft of the Classroom*. This was the book that my first headteacher gave to every new employee in his school:

> 'There is also a very understandable fear which many teachers have of losing the affection of pupils. This fear makes the teachers, like timid lovers, apprehensive lest the first dark look is evidence of favours withdrawn for ever... If your demand is legitimate and for the pupil's good, don't be tempted to abandon it. The relationships at which you should be aiming are those achieved by, say, the end of the year, not the end of the first week.'

The overly tentative teacher as a 'timid lover' is certainly a memorable image, if nothing else!

How is this magical notion of assertive presence attained before the students enter? Ideally by being present in the room, not rushing to a lesson, by having everything ready and in its place, and by a taking few deep breaths.

I have always also found it helpful to consider the classroom as 'my space', and that the students are therefore stepping into my 'home'. This gives any mock horror we might demonstrate when young people are not following our every instruction a sense of authenticity.

BE FIRST

For any teacher who is fortunate enough to have their own classroom, the initial priority is very clear: be there first.

A few years ago, I worked part-time for a year and therefore didn't have my own classroom in a large school that was split over two campuses in the North East of England. Stumbling across the school and arriving after students had already settled was hugely disconcerting. The most obvious drawback of this was that each lesson felt like it was me entering their space, not the other way around. This feeling has stuck with me since, and I place great value now on establishing that sense of calm and control that students will notice when they enter a room.

The welcome

We have already explored the importance of being at the door and welcoming students as they arrive, assessing the climate and establishing relationships. It is where that subliminal confidence and sense of ownership will come in: they are entering into your space and should be conscious of that.

By being at the door, we communicate that sense of ownership well. To reiterate this, the guidance from the Education Endowment Foundation (2021) is helpful:

> 'Recent research conducted with 11-14 year-olds suggests that greeting students positively at the classroom door is not only very low cost but has a high yield in terms of improving pupil behaviour in the classroom. Misbehaviour often occurs in schools around the start and end of lessons and when moving around the school building. By intentionally promoting and practising successful

> transitions into the classroom, teachers are empowered to help their students to be ready to learn. When delivered consistently, greeting pupils at the classroom door can help teachers to positively and personally connect with each student, deliver "pre-corrective" statements to remind students of class expectations, and deliver behaviour-specific praise. This strategy can be delivered by an individual teacher, but in secondary school in particular, there is likely to be an additional advantage to consistency at whole-school level.'

That entry should also speak of kindness and the importance of relationship development: by being there and warmly greeting them, we are placing a significant value on the importance of relationships to improve behaviour.

The way our classroom looks is also important: are they entering a space that is organised and clean or is it haphazard with chairs and tables all over the place? It might be appropriate to channel Marie Kondo here – 'the life-changing magic of tidying' indeed!

That entry into a suitable environment also needs to be balanced with clarity: what exactly are the expectations we have of our students that need to be communicated from the start?

1. Where do they put their bags, coats, etc.?
2. What do they need to take out? What do they need to put away?
3. What are the technology rules around phones, laptops, etc.?
4. What is the expectation about what they do when they sit down?
5. Is all this done in silence? What are the noise parameters?

These approaches will vary between schools and classes, but whatever that opening to a lesson is, it needs to be clear and ideally part of the routines you introduce in a classroom. If there are not routines established here, you can face an uphill battle to start the lesson in a brisk and proactive way.

Do Now tasks can be a helpful tool to ensure that the start of a lesson is used efficiently. This can be a few clear tasks that are outlined on a PowerPoint or written on the board that students are expected to start straight away. It can be something very simple or more creative and open-ended. This also serves the purpose of communicating that your classroom is a productive place and that no time is wasted in it. One they are working on that particular task, you can use the time to circulate and ensure that they have started well.

STARTING THE LESSON

The class are now sitting down (admiring your spruce cleanliness), they might have had a go at some sort of opening task, but now there is a general sense of anticipation: things need to start. To return to Michael Marland in his excellent *The Craft of the Classroom*, this can be challenging:

> 'Every moment of transition in the school day, every "start-up" generates inevitable tension and so is a possible source of trouble. Probably the most difficult of these moments is the arrival of the class, and probably the hardest of a secondary school teacher's jobs is the settling down of a class at the start of a new lesson.' (Marland, 1993)

Deep breath needed! Unless you are teaching in an idyllic paradise, the chances are the new class will not be sitting in rapt silence, desperate for you to kick things off in style. If they have to go through this transition six or seven times a day, the chances are they are in fact doing the opposite. It is more likely that there will be noise, rustling and the initial scanning the room for distractions.

You need to make a move.

The first move

That move is often a tentative 'OK, can you please be quiet?' that is instantly lost in the hubbub of general conversation and then repeated a number of times with increased desperation. Two simple errors are made here: the first is that your lovely polite request is asking the class rather than telling them, so the power dynamic instantly swerves into their hands. The 'please' is also too gentle, polite and weak in terms of what we need this opening gambit to be.

Ultimately, we need silence – not quiet – and we need it quickly so we can take control of the lesson. It requires us to channel some nervous energy into that magical teacher ingredient we explored earlier: presence.

We need to be skilful and seek a reframe that will be clear, confident and an imperative. One way to achieve this is to hold a central position of utter stillness; to resist every urge in our body to start moving around the room and putting out metaphorical fires. The second way we can do this is by introducing a countdown that gains the attention of the class.

The countdown

A countdown can be very helpful in managing a transition from a period of discussion to silence. The chances are if we ask for silence immediately it won't happen – it is human nature to bring our conversations to a natural close. A countdown can also be used to highlight positive behaviours, particularly when waiting for attention at the start of a lesson.

The volume can also range from a loud start with 'five' to a quieter finish with 'one'. Here is an example of securing attention at the start of a lesson:

> 'Five: attention on me, thanks.
>
> Four: excellent, thank you, Julie.
>
> Three: a couple of people still to respond.
>
> Two: and pens down, thanks.
>
> One: all eyes this way, thank you.'

It is all very simple and gives space for positive behavioural choices to be made, by clearly illuminating the expectations.

Focus phrases

If that doesn't work, we need to follow it with some key phrases, ensuring we pause after each to give the young people time to follow the instruction:

1. 'Settle down everyone, thank you.'
2. 'I'm ready to start, thank you.'

Each of these assertive options conveys control and authority. They are also positive in tone. There is no instant roar of anger or soiling of the atmosphere of the lesson. There is also, importantly, no arrogance – something that I think teenagers (like adults) can sense very quickly. It is arrogance, expressed through a sense of entitlement, that can be repellent in a classroom context. Less desirable personality traits like this can be magnified under the microscope of the classroom. (There is more on the power of 'thank you' to help work against this in the next chapter.)

This all sounds delightful, but is uttering one of these two magic phrases going to instantly quash the beginnings of a revolt in the room? Perhaps yes, but perhaps not. Either way, there is absolutely no way on earth that the lesson will begin without each and every one of them focused on you. If there is even the merest whisper and you decide to hedge your bets and go for it anyway, you are reinforcing that as a behavioural norm. Within weeks they will feel it is utterly acceptable to talk over you, and it will become an uphill battle.

Anonymity

At the start of the lesson, it is helpful to keep things as anonymous as possible. We don't want to instantly cause conflict with the more challenging students in the class by mentioning them by name. If our opening gambit doesn't work, you could employ one of the following phrases, maintaining a steely calm, a raised eyebrow and a general aura of 'you need to listen and engage now'.

1. '90% are beautifully focused and ready. I would like the last 10% to focus too, thank you.'
2. 'There are three people not focused yet. I am waiting.'

If students are in the 10% or are one of the three individuals, they know exactly who they are. The actual number of students not focusing may well be higher, but keeping the percentages and numbers low in your phrase establishes that paying attention is the behavioural norm in your classroom. That hopefully means the final few switch on and start to pay you attention. If they don't, another helpful one to establish attention is: 'We are going to do some really good stuff in the next 50 minutes. I'd like to start.' The fact that the learning is going to be wildly exciting gives them a reason to pay attention (it might not be wildly exciting, but I would always prefer to talk up a learning experience rather than talk it down!).

Once we have everyone – and that means absolutely *everyone* – with us, then we can give a chirpy 'good afternoon', 'good morning' or 'thank you for responding as I asked'. It is all deeply respectful, yet very clear.

Now, we will reflect in more detail on how different behavioural issues can be managed with our communication skills as the lesson progresses. It will be a balance of the body language strategies that we have reflected on previously, combined with some clear phrasing.

ARTICULATE THE STRUCTURE

How do we feel when we have no idea what the structure of a particular day will be? For some it can be quite liberating, but for others it can cause significant anxiety.

Consider how this feels in a morning of CPD. If the session is 'loose' and has no clear aim or direction, it can become very frustrating. It also makes us question the efficacy of the presenter – are they clear on where they are going? Or are we merely pawns in their rambling exploration of whatever they are trying to teach us?

In the classroom, this sense of structure is just as important. Teenagers need to feel both a sense of clarity and of comfort in our classroom settings, and to feel like they understand the direction a lesson is going in. The structure starts from the moment our students enter a classroom, with the expectations on how lessons will start.

Objectives

I don't feel it is essential to formally go through the learning objectives every lesson. Often this can be dry and result in more behavioural issues. I have also been in enough lessons to see that learning objectives are often flashed up, covered in about two seconds and then lost forever. What we do need to do, however, is give a crystal-clear explanation about what will happen in the lesson and what the core purpose of it is.

Some phrases you can use are:

- 'I'm really excited about today's lesson because we will be...'
- 'You will leave here in 50 minutes with...'
- 'What is the purpose of today's lesson? Well...'

It can also be much more creative by asking students to predict what the lesson will be about based on a few images or by getting them to set the objectives based on the past few lessons. This serves to generate curiosity, which will do more to manage the behaviour of a lesson than monotonous objectives that young people cannot make a connection with.

What will I be doing?

We have already covered the fact that teenagers (sometimes and understandably) can be more inclined towards self-absorption. Two central questions they will arguably have about lessons are 'what will I actually have to do in this lesson?' and 'how is this going to impact my life?' Feeding that self-interest can be helpful by clarifying what the outcomes of a lesson are and being clear on what students will need to produce. Again, it can be a rather formulaic approach: 'By the end of this lesson, you will have…'.

In central London I had a very challenging all-boy bottom-set Year 11 group in my NQT year, and my mentor suggested I do a checklist approach with them, which I have found very helpful since. The checklist was usually preprepared on the board and we would check it off together throughout the lesson. For example:

1. Read the first chapter of…
2. Collect quotations for…
3. Write a paragraph about the…

Clearly these aren't the most riveting of examples, but they certainly helped to give a sense of progress and clarity in the room. When the lesson wasn't going well (read 'often'), I could draw their attention to our checklist and convey my shock and sadness with phrases along the lines of: 'I'm really disappointed folks. We have still got two really important tasks we need to complete today.' It was also made crystal clear that if the tasks weren't completed, they would be done at home, at break, or lunchtime.

Success criteria

As well as knowing what they are in the lesson for and what they are expected to do, it is also helpful to explain how students can be successful in the lesson. What do they need to do in order to secure learning and progress in the lesson? As we discussed in the opening chapter, poor behaviour can often be the result of a lack of motivation. By being explicit about what they need to do in order to do something well, we can support our students to develop their enthusiasm for the lesson. Providing examples of excellence can help students attain success, and revealing a model of what they will need to do – Blue Peter style – can help. In English, this might be showing them an excellent example of a piece of creative writing.

Ron Berger, author of *An Ethic of Excellence*, writes about this:

> 'What is missing is clear: models. When young athletes work hard at their sport, they watch older students, Olympians, and professionals and imprint that vision in their hearts and minds. Unfortunately, when young students are engaged in academic work in school–creating a scientific report, persuasive essay, geometric proof, or architectural design–they typically have no idea of what would constitute excellence. They have no inspiration, no provocation, and no vision. We give students written assessment rubrics, but absent models of excellence, those rubrics are just a bunch of words. Picture the difference between reading a rubric of proficient play in soccer, and watching an Olympic soccer game.' (Berger, 2022)

By illuminating those aspirational standards for teenagers, we can allow them to attain the same clarity of excellence as they do when they study the amazing goals of Cristiano Ronaldo.

Timings

Timings can be very helpful to engender structure in a lesson and provide clarity, but they can also be overused. There is often a manic edge to a teacher who sets a class off on a task for 10 minutes then shouts every minute: 'You have nine minutes left!' or 'There are only eight minutes remaining' etc. There is clearly no need for teenagers to be reminded of this – they have the capacity to tell the time – and doing so both breaks concentration and adds to a loud atmosphere in a classroom.

A timer on the board is an excellent strategy where possible. It doesn't overwhelm students and helps to build metacognitive habits for planning and regulation that they will need for examinations. It quietly encourages focus and structure, and we can gesticulate silently towards it without interrupting students.

Routines

The habits that you embed in a classroom need to be clear to young people from the start. Again, it isn't the most exciting thing about being a teacher, but initially routines need to be repeated over and over again. They need to be practised relentlessly to ensure that everyone understands them. The magic word that you hear associated with any school that has managed to effectively tackle behaviour is 'consistency'.

One such routine that helps manage attention is to insist on teenagers having free hands when they are focused on you. It is important to have this conversation with any new classes to emphasise the importance of a routine and the rationale behind it: 'Why is it important that we are not fiddling with something when listening to me and each other?' Once the rationale is established this can be fairly simple to implement: 'Pens down, eyes on me, thanks.'

You will feel like a broken record with the number of times this needs to be repeated. It is a battle worth having though, and eventually, if the class know that you really mean it, they will start to self-govern this aspect of classroom life. One obsessive teacher-win can often make a real difference in the classroom – they become aware that you will not give in!

Sanctions

Sanctions will be given a chapter of their own later in this section of the book. Being utterly clear with young people about what the consequences will be if behaviour is poor is an important part of ensuring clarity in the classroom. What these are may well be school policy, but that should all be definite in any student's mind.

THANK YOU

How do you convey assertiveness in a room full of teenagers and maintain positive relationships? That is the challenge that all teachers have to face at some point. It is very easy to go too far either way: to be an authoritarian who seeks to force young people into behaving, whose method of communication could be described as being toxic, or to be the people pleaser we mentioned earlier, whose communication is limp and pleading.

For me, the answer arrives at the simple, yet gloriously polite, 'thank you'.

Is there a place for please?

Notice the difference between 'thank you' and its near cousin 'please'. Ultimately, 'please' doesn't convey the strength and conviction of a final 'thank you'. It implies that what you're saying is a request, rather than an instruction.

> 'Please stop talking, girls.'

Becomes:

> 'Stop talking girls, thank you.'

The impact of emphasis matters significantly here. In our first example, the girls hear 'please' first; in the second they here 'stop' first. Given some teenagers' capacity to switch off their hearing, the second sentence would have a much higher success rate. It implies a sense of trust and an expectation that the instruction will be followed without any protest. There is very limited opportunity for the girls, in this case, to argue.

That doesn't mean we should take a draconian approach and ban 'please' from our collection of teacher phrases. That would be ludicrous. 'Please' is a vital word – one that I am working hard to encourage my two young children to use! 'Yes, please' is a phrase that should dominate our language in the classroom:

> Student: 'Should we start?'
>
> Teacher: 'Yes, please.'
>
> Student: 'Shall I hand out the books, miss?'
>
> Teacher: 'Yes, please.'
>
> Student: 'Can I share my response, sir?'
>
> Teacher: 'Yes, please – that would be brilliant!'

Using 'yes please' in particular situations is great for building positive relationships and for encouraging young people to be proactive in the classroom.

Civility

Doug Lemov (2016) writes powerfully about the role of basic manners in securing positive behaviour:

> 'When society is in decay, "please" and "thank you" are the first things to go. It's useful to signal that civility and thus society are fully intact in your classroom by modelling "please" and "thank you" constantly, especially when students might see evidence of fraying.'

It is an interesting point to reflect deeper on. I know that when I am angry, my basic civility goes completely out of the window. For teenagers, these switches in emotion can happen very quickly, and result in very quick and capricious reactions. It is in fact extremely hard to sustain anger or irritation in the face of someone who is being unremittingly polite. Call workers are particularly inspiring on this front; they seem to be able to face a barrage of anger and still maintain an unruffled calm. Sarcasm is also a recipe for disaster when managing behaviour in the secondary context (with its connection to its near cousin mentioned earlier – arrogance), so maintaining a calm and polite manner is essential.

Sustaining decorum

The capacity to maintain that sense of decorum and calm in a classroom setting is hugely important. In this survival-of-the-fittest dynamic, teenagers thrive on getting some sort of reaction. I realise this is painting a savage picture of teenagers, but this chapter is about behaviour, so we should always assume the worst and be pleasantly surprised rather than the converse. My point, however, is that 'please' shouldn't be used when it comes to conveying authority and assertiveness with teenagers. If it is used in this context, it needs to be very distinct and very far from any sort of pleading. You can also use 'please' in a slightly menacing way with the emphasis placed more distinctly on the final word.

Saying 'thank you' is like a switch that helps us to maintain a business-like professionalism and calm. It means we will not match some of the more feral behaviour we are likely to face, and hopefully will make it clear exactly what we expect from young people.

Before we examine the range of behavioural issues we can face in the classroom, it is helpful to consider how our general use of language will help to prevent challenging behaviour. The first is to consider the ratio of our positive to negative language in the classroom.

THE LANGUAGE RATIO

Barbara Fredrickson, positive psychology professor and author of *Positivity*, has spent decades studying what will help humans flourish. She justifies her research and focus as follows:

> 'Far from being trivial, we've found that positive emotions broaden our awareness in ways that reshape who we are, and they build up our useful traits in ways that bring out the best in us, helping us become the best versions of ourselves.

> 'How to foster that mindset? It helps to be open, be appreciative, be curious, be kind, and above all, be real and sincere. From these strategies spring positive emotions.' (Fredrickson, 2009)

She writes about a 3:1 ratio, which argues for three positive moments for every negative one:

> 'By cultivating positive moments that make you feel optimistic, grateful, appreciated, inspired, awe-struck, and just plain happy, you can build your ability to enjoy life in general and seek out even more of these positive experiences.'

Now that sounds like an excellent recipe for being a teacher who is more inclined to be upbeat and enthusiastic, and to manage behaviour in a way that will help support young people. After all, striving to sustain a positive mindset and attitude is a key survival skill for working alongside teenagers!

Educational research also supports this. The Education Endowment Foundation highlights research that suggests a focus on a 5:1 ratio is effective:

'In another promising study, teachers in disruptive classes of pupils aged between 9 and 14 years old were trained over two 45-minute sessions to increase their use of behaviour-specific praise. Teachers were given reminders at intervals to praise students, alongside training focused on the 'magic 5:1 ratio' of positive-to-negative interactions. The 5:1 ratio theory is that for every criticism or complaint the teacher issues, they should aim to give five specific compliments, approval statements and positive comments or non-verbal gestures. This ratio has been shown to be key to long-lasting marriages and has been explored in other fields, such as medicine and business. Several interventions focusing on positive approaches to behaviour in classrooms promote this idea, but this research was the first experimental study to explore the feasibility and effectiveness of the approach. Over the two-month study, pupils increased their on-task behaviour by an average of 12 minutes per hour (or an hour per day), while pupils in similar comparison classes did not change their behaviour. This study implies that teachers with disruptive classes could benefit from increasing their positive interactions with pupils.' (EEF, 2021)

We have already considered the kind of teacher teenagers want to be taught by. It helps at this stage to remind ourselves of the nature of communication that some teenagers experience: negative media, negative self-perception and often negativity at home. As we explored earlier, we can either add to this diatribe of negativity or we can seek to offer a space that inclines much more deliberately towards positivity.

We want teenagers to make actively positive choices in our classrooms and to spurn the opportunity to indulge in negative behaviours. Therefore, the more their attention is directed towards positive choices, the more they are likely to feel that these are the behavioural norms in the room.

So how do we achieve it?

Mindset

The reality is that the calmer we are, and the more positive we feel before a lesson starts, the more likely we are to manifest such upbeat values for those who share our classroom spaces. How to achieve this level of calm will depend on the individual, although some commonalities will exist and help us all to feel confident, positive and calm: a clear lesson plan; an understanding of the individuals in the class; and channelling the passion and interest we have in our subjects.

The chapter on smiling earlier helps here: a smile in preparation helps us to feel positive before a lesson starts. We can combine this with a sense of acceptance – the lesson is very unlikely to go perfectly, and part of our mission in the classroom is being able to adapt and respond to the complex behaviours that teenagers will undoubtedly demonstrate. We also need to be very conscious of negativity bias and must not allow it to dominate our thinking.

The negativity bias

The more aware we are of the negativity bias, the less likely we are to fall into its seductive allure. It is an innate part of our human psyche that causes us to focus on the more negative aspects of our lives, rather than the more positive ones. This inclination is revealed by considering what happens if we are driving and on one side of the road is a car accident and the other side is a beautiful waterfall. Our attention is almost always held by the car accident – a fact that is ruthlessly exploited by the extensive negative news in the media. It is a by-product of evolution: our ancestors needed this in order to focus on immediate threats and avoid being eaten by giant tigers. In the classroom, it can often be counterproductive, making us hypervigilant about the numerous threats that can face us.

Observing the tendency to think negatively is a useful starting point. We then need to supercharge the rational side of our brain in order to counter such thinking. We can challenge negative thinking by gently reminding ourselves why the internal thinking we are going through might not necessarily be a true reflection of the events.

We need to be careful that we are not lowering our expectations by applying this positivity ratio – we are not going to praise young people merely for looking at us.

Name the specific behaviours

In order to keep the positive ratio high in the classroom, we need to name the specific behaviours that are contributing to a positive atmosphere.

Being clear about our classroom values helps here – what do we really want to shine a light on?

For me, much of that is about being attentive, respectful and thinking carefully. Any opportunity to be explicit about students showing those qualities helps. However, it also helps to know our students before we publicly celebrate them. Some students will find this excruciatingly embarrassing, and a quiet word of praise is going to be much more effective for them:

- 'Thank you, John, you are being really attentive.'
- 'I love how carefully you are listening, Mary.'
- 'You are working really hard today, Aziz, thank you.'
- 'You thought so carefully about that, Matthew. Thank you for taking the time to do that.'

Name the benefits

A spotlight on positive behaviour can also illuminate the benefits of those behaviours. At times that can be a class conversation: when discussing effective listening, for example, we can highlight the effect that being able to listen well has on our lives (improved relationships, empathy, compassion, less self-absorption etc.). Those benefits can be made even more explicit by thinking of ways you can reinforce positive behavioural norms in the classroom. How often do classroom displays have an inadvertent focus on negative behaviour, such as those that display class rules and sanctions? Changing the displays in your classroom to outline your vision of what an excellent student does (rather than what they shouldn't do) can help build positive behavioural norms.

Avoiding judgement

I've fallen into a habit when I find out I have a new class. I scurry around the English department asking for feedback on my new students. I even write little annotations on a seating plan. If the teacher tells me that little Billy is 'a nightmare – he never stops talking', then my perception of Billy is fixed from the start. I am hyperaware of him, almost internally inviting him to start talking in the first few lessons.

Teenagers respond differently to different environments, so reserving judgement of them is a vital component to maintaining a positive manner with them in the classroom. I have lost count of the number of times I have been delightfully surprised when that 'nightmare' student never manifests and my preconceptions have been entirely unjustified.

There is a famous Native American story that strikes me as encapsulating the ideas in this chapter perfectly.

> One evening, an old Cherokee tells his grandson that inside all people, a battle goes on between two wolves. One wolf is negativity: anger, sadness, stress, contempt, disgust, fear, embarrassment, guilt, shame, and hate. The other is positivity: joy, gratitude, serenity, interest, hope, pride, amusement, inspiration, awe and, above all, love.
>
> The grandson thinks about this for a minute, then asks his grandfather, 'Well, which wolf wins?'
>
> The grandfather replies, 'The one you feed.'

Let's return to that all-boy bottom-set Year 11 class in central London. I can't say it was all a glorious success, but I did have more success when I realised that my persona could make such a difference to my lessons. Many of them had enough shouting and negativity surrounding them from challenging home lives, as well as media and cultural influences. Coming into my lessons had been providing them more of the same.

The parable speaks of the kind of person young people want to be in a room with: teachers who are calm and positive, and who demonstrate gratitude, joy and laughter. By reframing our thinking to quietly manage challenging behaviour and loudly exclaim the positives in our lessons, it goes some way in building a class community in which positivity, optimism and effort are celebrated and heralded.

A classroom, that is, where we feed the second wolf.

LANGUAGE TO DEPERSONALISE BEHAVIOUR

We have established that teenagers can be reactive, and some are wired to respond with hostility. Being sensitive to those fluctuations in behaviour is key, and one of our language aims in the classroom should be to make sure that behaviour is depersonalised as far as possible. The connotations of 'depersonalised' are not particularly positive, suggesting coldness and a lack of individuality. In the context of managing behaviour in our classrooms, the key is finding a dispassionate response to difficult situations so that we don't appear to be attacking the teenager's personality. Yes, we want to raise their behavioural awareness and make positive steps in improving it – but we don't want to seem like we are attacking them personally.

To illustrate what that means, it is useful to consider what it looks like when we are using a more personalised method of managing behaviour.

Personalised behaviour management

'He totally hates me.' I'm sure I'm not the only one who has walked down a school corridor and heard a teenager (often very persuasively) outlining the reasons why a teacher has a vendetta against them. Perhaps it is true, perhaps not – but by convincing themselves of the truth of a teacher's dislike, this young person has given themselves a get-out-of-jail-free card so they don't have to take any responsibility for their behavioural choices in the classroom. In fact, they are well on the way to justifying why they won't even try to do the work in that lesson – they think blame lies entirely with the teacher. They will also be on the lookout for evidence to support their claim. Evidence we clearly can't afford to fuel them with.

This is one of the hardest self-regulation aspects of working with teenagers. Of course, some teenagers will be remarkably hard to 'like', and we may dread the moment they come bounding into our classrooms to cause havoc. They, however, must never get a sense of this internal struggle we are experiencing, and instead they need to feel unconditional positive regard and professional detachment from us. We need to remain, at all times, the mature adult in the room.

So how does a teenager arrive at the view that a teacher 'hates' them? Let's consider some phrases that would add to this teenager's sense of outrage.

The rhetorical question

Using a rhetorical question in an attempt to tackle off-task behaviour, is a trap we have all fallen into:

- 'Why are you still talking?'
- 'What are you doing out of your seat?'
- 'Why are you always so disruptive?'
- 'What is wrong with you today?'
- 'Why are you calling out again?'

All of these examples have a significant degree of hostility attached to them – they imply real frustration at the presence of the teenager. The pronoun 'you' adds to this, by attaching it personally to the individual. Phrases such as the above are also, in reality, utterly pointless – they don't signal that talking should stop and they aren't clear about what we do want to see.

There is also no real way to answer them in a positive way or without adding to the conflict. They also send messages of a lack of control to the rest of the class, implying we haven't got the assertive tools necessary to manage the behaviours, and even hint of desperation.

Shut up

There are variations of this, but telling a teenager to 'shut up' is an example of deviating from a mature and dispassionate way to manage classroom behaviour. It is, sadly, also more common than we might think. It also has the potential to provoke instant feelings of anger from the recipient in response and clearly displays a sense of dislike towards a young person. This kind of interaction can fuel feelings of resentment in a young person and cause them to harbour feelings of revenge.

If we tell a teenager to shut up, it is clear that we don't have the capacity to regulate our emotions, potentially sparking an adrenaline-filled confrontation that will inevitably lead to more issues. This kind of phrase will completely derail learning for the entire class. Their attention is now captivated by you and the individual, as they eagerly wait for the situation to develop. It adds a drama to the classroom that we can definitely do without.

Shouting

In response to noise and disruption in a lesson, there is often a temptation to match the volume. At times it can seem to work and lead to some instant passivity, but that passivity is created only because it is often what some young people are used to hearing at home. Regardless of the initial response, shouting only ever leads to a temporary change in behaviour. Before long the environment will be exactly the same. Unfortunately, I have definitely been there!

There is an interesting societal point to raise here: would we accept people in other professions shouting at us? How would we feel if the dentist started shouting at our children? Roaring at a young person in an army commander style serves only one purpose: shattering a relationship. It is communication at its most primal and unsophisticated. It can also generate a huge amount of emotion in a teenager – the likely result being that they begin to tune out from things you say. It can also be very triggering for teenagers and return them to difficult points in their life. The frequency of this in the Teen Talk feedback that opens this section is revealing.

There might be moments when we explore raising the volume of our voice in a controlled way, but explicitly shouting at an individual is ultimately unskilled and harmful. It creates a dark and ominous cloud over a classroom and it can be hard to regain control. Our position as a role model can be challenged. Instead, we need to find as many examples as possible to model confidence and calm in even the most emotionally fuelled moments – moments that demonstrate that teenagers will not get a reaction from their usual patterns of behaviour.

Body language

We have noted already how pervasive body language is in the classroom. In communicating with young people about behaviour, it becomes even more important. If we seek to use body language to intimidate a young person – if we stand over them and look down at them – we reinforce an impression that we are somehow better than them.

Paul Dix, author of *When the Adults Change, Everything Changes*, writes well about the importance of this:

> 'It is often said that getting down to students' eye level is important when delivering praise or sanctions to students. This can often be interpreted as leaning over a student rather than standing above them or sitting down next to them. I often observe teachers who think they are at the student's eye level but are actually still demanding that the student looks up at them. I prefer the student to be looking down at me; teachers who do this know that crouching down lower than eye level is not weak but assertive and confident physical language.' (Dix, 2010)

Address the behaviour not the teenager

In order to avoid a breakdown of the relationships we cultivate with young people, we should focus on the behaviours they are demonstrating and not on them as an individual. Detaching the behavioural feedback from their personalities means that there is not the same personal investment. Let's consider some phrases:

> 'Billy, today I'd like to see you working as well as you did yesterday. Make a positive choice and stop talking, thank you.'

This sort of corrective feedback begins with praise, reminding the young person that they are perfectly capable of making positive choices in the lesson. It is also very clear that they know what the expectations are (that they curb their talking) and that doing so is connected with them making a positive choice. The instructional nature of the sentence is very short and clear, balanced with language that is much more positive.

The phrase 'make a positive choice' is one of my favourites in the classroom. It highlights to the young person that their poor behaviour at this stage is an active choice – and it is within their power to rectify it. It also keeps the positive language ratio high and can be used in many ways.

Consider this alternative interaction with Georgia:

> 'You are being a nightmare today. Why are you still talking?'

Note what happens when we don't even use a child's name – it conveys a lack of investment in both the relationship and an attempt to calm them down. The use of 'nightmare' is also symptomatic of the negative way some teachers discuss young people and can seep into classroom interactions. Its connotations are clear to a teenager: a nightmare is something we would do anything to escape from.

Considering how it feels to be on the receiving end of this interaction is revealing. There is also very little you can say in response. Let's consider an alternative:

> 'Georgia, your choices today are making it difficult for you to concentrate. The work today is important and I'd really like you to have a go at it.'

As we mentioned earlier, saying a young person's name has a calming impact and a relational one. The structure of this sentence is also important, with the focus on 'choices' and the negative impact they are having on her learning. It leads us on to perhaps the most important way to depersonalise behaviour: to focus on the work rather than the student.

Focus on the work

Teenagers are in our classrooms for one core purpose: to learn. In order to learn, they need to be engaged and to translate the learning into some kind of outcome. Behaviour management in the classroom should always come back to the work, not the individual. It can be a useful way to reframe attention and behaviour in a classroom to begin with the work.

In this scenario, there are two boys discussing last night's Champions League football game rather than working. The focus on the work should be in the opening question:

> 'Gentlemen, how are you getting on with the essay?'

Instead of starting the conversation by acknowledging the poor behaviour, the attention is drawn to the essay they should be writing. Inevitably, the 'gentlemen' in question will at this point look down at their work rather sheepishly. Now is our moment to address the behaviour:

> 'I'm disappointed not to see much writing. It looks like you are struggling to focus. Do I need to move your seats?'

The focus again remains on the work – not the fact that they are being menaces. The question here isn't rhetorical. We can wait with a raised eyebrow for a response. They will, of course, say no. That can be followed with:

> 'OK. I'm looking forward to coming back in 10 minutes and seeing how much you have written.'

They know you will be back and hopefully they will put their heads down. If you come back and they haven't completed any work, they will be moved.

There are many other phrases you can use to maintain focus on the work:

- 'Can you show me how much work you have completed today?'
- 'Do you have any questions about the work today?'
- 'You were flying yesterday, Liam, and completed so many questions. What is happening today?'
- 'I'm really looking forward to marking your book, Georgia. Are you trying as hard as you can today?'

This can also be balanced with silent body language: an inclination of the head towards a young person's work; a pointed finger that draws the attention towards the work; or even just looking down at a workbook or jotter.

Use 'I'

In this mission to depersonalise behaviour, it is important that our tone does not become aggressive or confrontational. Using 'you' can make teenagers feel victimised:

- 'You aren't doing any work again!'
- 'You need to stop talking.'
- 'You will be kept behind again…'

Instead, it is helpful to use 'I' in order to refocus the attention on your response to the behaviour the teenager is demonstrating. 'I've noticed' is my personal favourite here, helping to show your ownership of the behaviour and how it is demonstrated. It is also without judgement – merely an observation without comment.

The above phrases become:

- 'I've noticed that you haven't completed as much work as yesterday. Why is that? I'm ready to listen.'
- 'I've noticed you are talking again. Can you refocus – thank you.'
- 'I've noticed you are a bit distracted today. I really don't want to have to keep you behind after the lesson.'

The final part of the first example is important. If we ask for a reason why the teenager is demonstrating poor behaviour, then we need to be ready to listen to the response. That requires giving the young person time, then responding appropriately to what they bring up. More often than not they will point out struggles with the work at this point. If they don't and they start to head off on a tangent, an excellent counter is 'that may be so, but right now I need you to…'. That cuts off any possible debate or argument and refocuses them on the work we need them to do.

Holding grudges

Every lesson with a teenager should signal a new opportunity. While that sentence is easy to write, I know all too well how challenging it is to enact. One of the positive aspects of working in a secondary school, however, is that there is an opportunity for space and reflection at the end of each lesson, for both the teacher and the student. Primary teachers who have challenging students all day are blessed with superhuman patience and have my utmost respect!

In an ideal world, if there are serious issues in a lesson, there should be some kind of restorative conversation before the students come back into the classroom. Often, however, this isn't the case, and a teenager returns to your classroom without any intervention despite a poor previous lesson. A sense of a new start should be communicated in a positive way with a young person when they enter the classroom. They should feel they are entering a space in which they are welcomed and celebrated (even if this does require from us some Oscar-winning acting).

- 'I'm really looking forward to seeing you working well today, Zelda.'
- 'Let's have a brilliant lesson from you today, Jon.'
- 'Great to see you, Bob. We are going to do some great stuff today.'

We need to find opportunities to intentionally repair the relationship when there has been conflict or poor behaviour. That involves being explicit about our care for the student and a desire to start again. It might involve some kind of mutual problem solving, such as having a discussion together about what might work best moving forwards.

The reality is that what rests on the success of these strategies is interpersonal communication, recognising that the words we use, and how we use them, have the potential to impact young people in front of us. None of us are perfect, and we will make mistakes in our interactions in the classroom – like all aspects of teaching, however, it is about constant reflection and learning from those mistakes.

MOBILE PHONES

For such small and innocuous-looking things, mobile phones have the potential to completely shatter concentration in a classroom. We all know how addicted we can be as adults to our mobiles, but this problem is compounded when it comes to the relationships that teens have with their phones.

Research

In 2018, France decided to completely ban mobile phones from the classroom. There are a range of interesting studies that appear to support such a strong principle:

> 'For example, a recent study found that UK schools who banned mobile phones saw a 6.4% increase in their students' grades, with this effect being particularly pronounced amongst struggling students. In another fascinating study, students separated into two groups were taught the same lesson, but only one of the groups had access to electronics (phones and laptops). Those who had been allowed to use electronics performed 5% worse in the final exam than the other group who had no access to this technology.' (Innerdrive, 2022)

We might work in a school where phones are banned – if so, brilliant, we can gleefully skip past this chapter, snorting with derision at our poor teaching colleagues who have to engage in the Battle of the Mobile every day.

In most contexts in the UK, teenagers will still have phones in their possession. Some schools will insist on them being switched off and in teenagers' bags, but the chances of that actually happening are slim. The reality is that you are likely to have to tackle students either furtively checking their phones in their pockets or brazenly taking them out during lessons.

Have a conversation

It is vital we engage teenagers in conversations about mobile phone usage and addictive behaviour. To not reference mobile phones is to ignore the gigantic elephant in the room. Arguably, we also have a moral responsibility to educate young people on the ways in which they are being influenced by social media companies who exploit them for money.

There are also the myths about multitasking and the negative impact it can have on sleep. There are many aspects that will counter the arguments that teenagers are likely to make about phones being vital for their wellbeing. Having conversations about phones with teenagers can be very positive and can be explored in the context of attention and the purpose of classrooms. That can be initiated by exploring a couple of questions:

1. What role should mobile phones play in our lessons?
2. What issues do you see with mobile phones being part of lessons?

This initial conversation can then lead to the clear rules about mobile phones that you want to impose in your classroom. This may be dictated by school policy, but whatever the guidance is, it should be very clear.

School policy

Ideally, you will work in a school that has very clear expectations around mobile phone usage. The reality is that in our modern era schools really need to be a step ahead. That makes the classroom teachers' communication about mobile phones really simple: 'You know what the school rules are, Michael. I need your mobile to stay in your bag.'

Be observant

Something else that teenagers are remarkably skilled at is the ability to avoid detection when on mobile phones. We need to make sure that we are carefully monitoring all aspects of the classroom to check for mobile phone usage. Previous points about eye contact and positioning in the classroom are important here – make sure there are no blind spots that young people can exploit.

Sometimes that observation can be preventative enough. We may just stare at a young person who is having a sneaky wee check of their mobile and that can make them aware that it is unacceptable. They will most likely return the phone to their bags.

Give choices

The mobile choice conundrum can be a good one:

> 'Bob, I've noticed you have taken your phone out. You can either put it away or it will be confiscated.'

Hopefully this is following the school rules, so there is no confrontation that can occur. We then walk away, giving Bob some take-up time to make up his mind about what he needs to do. Back at the front of the room, we turn our steely and confident gaze to him, presuming that he has made the right choice. If he hasn't, we swoop and grab the phone, placing it on eBay to make ourselves a small fortune. Perhaps.

INITIATE A SURVEILLANCE STATE

I appreciate the title of this is somewhat big-brotherish. Let's be clear: implementing cameras to watch young people's every move in the classroom is probably going a tad too far. The sentiment, however, is true: we need to have eyes all over every aspect of our classrooms.

A huge part of managing behaviour is keeping a step ahead and tracking the room to keep abreast of potential issues.

To return to Michael Marland:

> 'An important part of classroom technique is maintaining a constant surveillance of everything that is happening in the room. This means that the teacher's position in the room needs thought, as does the posture in which he helps a pupil.' (Marland, 1993)

The look

Sustaining eye contact with a teenager who is clearly about to make some wrong decisions is often enough to stop them. It needs to speak, again, of assertive confidence – an arched eyebrow and a look that makes it absolutely clear that you won't tolerate whatever menacing they are about to indulge in.

Soon, the class will know that you have that unique capacity that only the most revered of teachers have: you know everything that is going on in the classroom before it happens. They will surreptitiously turn to try to make sure they can do something and be met only by your calm and assertive eyes.

Positioning

We have explored this already, but one of the mistakes I made at the start of my teaching career was not standing still at the front of the room. I would set young people off on a task then sprint Usain-Bolt-style into the mix. I then watched a masterful maths teacher and saw how he always waited after setting his students a task. He paused and explicitly told the teenagers, 'I'm just going to make sure everyone is focused, then I will come around the room. Lovely level of focus, folks.' It was so simple and so positive. His class knew that he was watching and avoided drifting into off-task conversations. It mopped up any wasted time and prevented conflict.

Not having our back to the class is also important. We must make sure that at all times we have visibility of the whole class. This again is fairly unnatural and can be tiring, but it is a vital part of tracking students' progress.

Circulation

We have already explored the notion of confident ownership when it comes to behaviour. Adam Riches has blogged on the importance of not hiding behind the desk when it comes to managing the classroom:

> 'I work with a lot of trainee teachers and they use the desk at the front of the class in a novel way. It is used as a kind of barricade between themselves and the class – it provides them with a physical wooden barrier that they often feel (initially at least) gives them some protection from the rabid horde in front of them.

> 'Of course, they quickly come to realise that standing behind their desk inhibits them from truly dominating the front of the classroom and as their confidence grows, they venture out from their safe place into the realms of the unknown.' (Riches, 2019)

Making sure there are no hidden areas in the classroom is important in this regard. Instead, there is a need to be visible in all the corners of a room – to make sure we get around every desk and acknowledge every student. This also helps us to build positive relationships with all the various personalities that will be sharing our classroom space with us.

That doesn't happen by magic. We need to make sure we track and plan out how we move around our classroom spaces. Otherwise, we float meaninglessly from student to student. Riches continues to outline how we might go about achieving this productive circulation:

'Observing is not watching – observing means looking at practice and calculating your next actions. While a teacher circulates the class, they need to make a note (mentally or physically) of what needs addressing or re-addressing in order for the class to improve. By effectively tracking misconceptions and successes, teaching becomes responsive and learning is more efficient.'

MANAGING SECONDARY BEHAVIOURS

We have clarified that there are many attention-seeking behaviours that teenagers demonstrate in the classroom and that they often have a desire to secure peer approval. This chapter will attempt to address the question: how much should we strategically ignore, and how much should we tackle?

It is always an internal battle in a lesson: whether or not we should address certain actions or comments. Let's consider this example: David has been chatting to his friend Josh about the latest *Love Island* adventures. You go over, talk to him about his work and remind him of the level of focus you require for him to do his work well – and suggest that he should perhaps leave exploring *Love Island* until break. As you walk away, he tuts loudly and says to his friend: 'I can't stand him. What an arse!' You instantly feel your face flush and feel a wave of anger. Do you address it with him in this moment?

There are really no benefits to be found in creating a confrontation in the heat of this adrenaline-filled moment. All it will do is give David the audience that he wants, and validate him in front of his friend. This, to be clear, is exactly what he wants. He doesn't really think you are an 'arse' – the reality is he is probably fairly apathetic to you as a human being – but he wants to create a scenario where he is validated by his peers.

It is in this kind of moment that we need to take a deep breath, pause and recognise that this is not a useful moment to approach the conversation. Catching David at the end of the lesson as he leaves, and being clear that you heard him, might be a better approach: 'David, I was really let down by your comment to Josh earlier. I care about you doing well in my lessons and would like us to have a positive relationship.'

This makes it clear to him that you are human, have emotions, and that you value your relationship with him. The focus is again on learning and a shared purpose that underpins your relationship with him. There needs to be a focus on treating each other with dignity in the classroom, and that common respect also applies to conversing with the teacher. Without his chum with him, and now that the moment has passed, the likelihood is that David will feel suitably remorseful and offer an apology.

If he doesn't show some kind of conciliatory behaviour, this is the moment where we need to get into something that has been missing so far from this section: the use of sanctions. Relationship building, however, comes first – we need to stage the sanctions so that their use is appropriate. This will be the focus of the next chapter, but here it would be useful to follow up with either of the following:

- 'If I hear that kind of comment again, I will need to have a conversation with your parents.'
- 'It is really important that we are respectful to each other in my classroom. If you speak to me like that again, I will unfortunately have to you remove you from the classroom.'

Note the use of 'if' in each example, which is where the emphasis should be in the sentence. This reiterates to the teenager that they ultimately have to make the choice in the classroom.

There are other secondary behaviours that are less dramatic, but dominate in every classroom across the country:

1. **The exaggerated sigh.** Teenagers are experts at this – I'm confident many of them gather together with their chums and practise for hours. You could froth at the mouth and ask: 'Is there a reason you are sighing at me?' and get into a useless dialogue about the merits of sighing. Or you could ignore it completely, recognising that some teenagers have a sighing affliction that you will never be able to fight against.

2. **'This is so boring.'** The 'so' is usually elongated to comic effect, and it is often coupled with an exaggerated head or hand gesture. We could get into a debate with our teenage chum and engage in a heated discussion about why studying the poem 'The Road Not

Taken' is in fact going to change their life and make them approach life decisions more much profoundly in the future – but it is an argument we are very unlikely to win. Instead, a simple 'OK' or 'thank you for the feedback' before moving on very swiftly will keep the pace of the lesson up and prevent any off-task discussion. It is helpful to also avoid the word 'but', which has negative connotations. 'I can see you think it is boring, **and** I would like you to finish the work that has been set.' It doesn't start an argument and keeps things very calm and clear.

Having scripts for the above scenarios will save us time and keep the focus on learning in our classrooms. They all need to be balanced, however, with the judicious use of sanctions.

SANCTIONS

Some people in teaching bristle at the word 'sanction': will it shatter relationships and crush the self-esteem of young people? Should it be replaced with a focus on restorative conversations? The reality is that a lot of that well-meaning thinking is from individuals who have not taught in challenging schools, or with challenging teenagers.

I don't believe in punitive sanctions for the sake of them, but firmly believe that there needs to be consequences for misbehaviour in the classroom. Having taught in a sanction-free school for a few months, I have had very clear experience of what happens to behaviour when there are no consequences for the choices that teenagers make. Flashbacks still often appear in my dreams!

There is no doubt that excessive use of sanctions will be counter-intuitive, negatively impacting relationships and learning. That is why they only appear now in this dialogue about how to use communication to secure positive behaviour in classrooms. Instead, we should see them as yet another means to ensure a productive and positive atmosphere in our classrooms. Using sanctions is about making sure that young people have consequences for their actions in our classrooms. We must also consider how to repair and rebuild relationships when sanctions do have to be issued.

Clarity

The sanctions might be a whole-school or departmental policy, so it is likely that we won't have much ownership over the decisions about them. In order for them to be used effectively, however, we need to be absolutely clear about what they are supposed to be issued for and to what severity.

For them to really work, there needs to be utter transparency and clarity of communication across a school. Young people need to hear and see the same messages over and over again, with no variations according to either subject or teacher.

Stages of sanctions

All behavioural feedback in a classroom should be given in stages. We have explored how a quiet conversation that refocuses the young person on their work is always the first stage. This will result in a number of teenagers re-engaging. For a minority, however, it is naive to think that a quiet word will be all they need in the lesson to ensure focused behaviour. Sanctions may well need to be used to make sure that undesired behaviour is not repeated.

Conflict often occurs in classrooms. However, when teenagers feel that the sanction has arrived magically from nowhere. It results in an instantly inflammatory response: 'That is so unfair!' Instead of reaching for an epic detention straight away, we instead follow the following steps that allow us to stage opportunities for the student to correct their behaviour.

Explain the sanction

Before any sanction is applied, there should be an opportunity for the young person to rectify their behaviour. That might be a warning explaining that a sanction will be applied if their behaviour does not change: 'I really don't want to have to keep you at break, Burhana, so I need to see another paragraph written.' Phrases like this make it clear that we do not want to issue sanctions, which helps us maintain positive relationships with our students. They imply certainty and respect, whereas if we instantly launch into publicly berating a teenager, that respect is easily lost.

Once we have explained what the sanction might be, we walk away and allow the teenager to make up their own mind about the direction of their behaviour, implying that we trust them to take responsibility.

Make sanctions reasonable

In order for the relationship and respect to be sustained, sanctions need to be appropriately applied. Inevitably, teenagers will sulk and cry out 'that isn't fair' when they receive a sanction, but we need to be able to rationalise why it is fair. We should use a calm statement that explains clearly why they have been issued with a sanction, avoiding the pull to give some sarcastic response at all costs:

- 'I appreciate you are upset. The reason why...'
- 'I can see that you disagree...'

Phrases like these validate the teenager and prevent the situation from escalating further. Doing this quietly in the classroom away from their peers is also important – we never want to give poor behaviour an audience.

Students leaving the room

A group of students gathered in the corridor is never a good move: it becomes a means for them to show off to their chums that they have been kicked out – and an opportunity to have a good rant about the teacher.

It can, however, prove to be a good chance to allow a teenager to cool off and provides a quiet space removed from peers for you to have behavioural conversations. As a rule, however, time outside should be kept brief. The teenager who often finds themselves stood in a corridor instead of engaging in lessons is not only missing valuable learning time, but is building further resentment and evidence that their teacher doesn't value them.

Follow up

Teenagers are remarkably adept at avoiding sanctions. They seem to have an innate ability to disappear off the face of the earth when the word 'detention' is uttered. This vanishing act can often leave us looking completely ineffectual and unable to take ownership over classroom behaviour. That is why we need to be utterly obsessive about sanctions being completed.

There will be a range of outlandish and creative excuses as to why the sanction cannot be completed: 'But sir, I was getting my nails done!' was one of my favourite reasons a teenager gave for not attending a detention. None, however, should count. Any decent head of department or school leadership team will also support this obsessive need for sanctions to be completed.

After we have mastered sanctions, the next challenge is to engage with parents. That in itself, however, can be more complex than we might assume.

PARENTAL COMMUNICATION

They can be our best friends or our biggest enemies in our quest to secure positive behavioural choices: parents and carers. For the purposes of clarity, for the rest of this chapter I will refer to them as parents (plural) – but that comes with an understanding and appreciation it may be a single parent or carer who is looking after the teenager.

In my naive early days of teaching, I believed that by phoning home I would instantly have little Jimmy behaving in my lessons, but it isn't usually as simple as that. Indeed, that initial phone call with little Jimmy's parents went terribly wrong, with me somehow managing to isolate and offend both him and his parents.

What can we expect if we engage parents in conversations about behaviour? While the vast majority of parents will be superb and will want to do everything they can to support us in making sure their son or daughter is behaving in our lessons, there are some conversations that, for whatever reason, prove more complex.

It is perhaps helpful at this stage to illustrate some of the reasons why parental conversations can prove challenging.

Defensiveness

Little Jimmy, to return to my earlier example, was in fact an angel at home and in every other aspect of his life (apparently). His father asked me to seriously reflect on my teaching abilities and not blame his little cherub.

Some parents do not believe that their children are misbehaving. There might be a range of reasons for that, and it is absolutely not up to us to pass judgement – nor would it be a positive use of our time. It would be counter-intuitive to have a conversation about a teenager's behaviour with no evidence to support our claims. More on that to come.

Lack of ownership

'I'm so sorry, I just don't know what to do with her.' This is another refrain that can echo in conversations with parents – particularly with teenage parents. Again, for many complex reasons, the parents may be struggling in the same way we are in the classroom – to take control over their child's behaviour.

It can be difficult when we are seeking help from parents to support the message we are giving the young person: the parents might not be able to reinforce our work in the classroom.

What can we do?

It is clear that engaging with parents can be a very worthwhile conversation. It shows the teenager that you are really committed to them making positive behavioural choices in your lessons and that it is worth you investing time in communicating with their parents. Teenagers, of course, are not all likely to see it that way – particularly if the conversation is not a positive one. The first step in securing proactive and helpful relationships with parents is to tap back into the focus on positive psychology that has dominated this book: start with the bright spots.

When I was a very earnest NQT, I made the point of phoning up all the parents of my more challenging classes in the first few weeks. I wouldn't advocate this approach now – it took hours. But it made a real difference in supporting behaviour in the classroom at the start of the year. The script went like this:

> 'Hello there, I am Jimmy's new English teacher. I am just phoning to introduce myself. I also just wanted to say what a brilliant start Jimmy has made to the school year: I am really enjoying teaching him.'

The response to the opening sentence is often revealing, with many parents interjecting before you can give the positive feedback. You often hear something along the lines of, 'Oh no, what has he/she done now!' It shows just how few positive communications these parents have received about their child, and is perhaps indicative of the style of parental communication that is prioritised in schools.

In the modern era, I think a telephone call is hugely appreciated by parents, but it doesn't have to be via the phone. Sending an email can be just as powerful. You also don't have to do the whole class – a handful of positive phone calls or emails can be very helpful in the first few weeks. It can also be a lovely thing to do at the end of the week on a Friday, sending out a few emails to parents of pupils who have tried hard during the week.

It means that the first interaction you have with a parent isn't negative and isn't about to set up a conflict. It may well be that a more challenging phone call has to take place later in the year, and for that call you have some positive resonance to rely on.

Behaviour issue phone call

Having banked our positive phone call, we can now turn our attention to the more challenging calls. Let's imagine that Jimmy (my sincere apologies if your name is Jimmy – I realise you may feel somewhat victimised by this chapter!) has been presenting some behavioural issues – in this case, he is very distracted and lacking in focus. How do we approach the call to make sure it can positively impact his behaviour in the classroom?

The first consideration is to make sure that we are not alienating either him or his parents. We therefore start on a positive:

> 'Hello there, it's Jimmy's English teacher. We spoke earlier this year about what a great start Jimmy has made. While I still really enjoy teaching Jimmy, some of his behavioural choices have been less positive in the last few weeks. I'd really like to explore with you how we can get back to more of what I saw at the start of the year.'

We might not, at this stage, love being in the same room as young Jimmy, but his parents don't need to know that. We also don't need to launch into some diatribe about what an utter nightmare Jimmy is because he just can't keep his mouth shut and is ruining all our lessons. Instead, we need to follow the classic communication guidance to 'sandwich' the feedback we give to his parents.

Ask questions

Nobody likes to sit through a long monologue, so asking parents questions about how their child is feeling about the subject is important. It also helps us to identify possible reasons that might explain behavioural choices:

- 'How does Jimmy feel about his lessons?'
- 'Is there anything I need to know about that might be influencing Jimmy's behavioural choices in the classroom?'

Some of the answers to these questions might not be particularly helpful ('Jimmy finds biology really boring/Jimmy thinks you pick on him', etc.), but at least it is allowing space for dialogue and for you to demonstrate that you are listening and reflecting on the needs of their child.

Evidence

We need to have evidence to support the fact that Jimmy isn't working in our subject and is misbehaving. If the meeting is in person, having his workbook/jotter with us to talk through can help. It is often beneficial if we use this sensitively alongside the work of a student who is more focused.

Doing a quick check with his other subjects can help too – sending an email is an easy way to achieve this. All it takes is for others to send a one-liner about his attitude in their lessons to prevent accusations that Jimmy is excellent in all his other subjects. There are also usually behavioural systems (merits/demerits) that can be checked and used to support these difficult conversations. The main point is to make sure you have evidence for any claims you might be making.

What do we want?

Before we make the phone call, we need to be clear about what we want the outcome to be. Clearly it is, in part, a general conversation about expectations – but that might end up being a fairly meaningless chat. Do we want parental permission to hold Jimmy back in detentions? Supportive parents are usually on side with this – 'You do what you have to!'. Or do we want to put him on some kind of behavioural report? Do we want to open up regular channels of communication with them?

Polite

I have also found that being unfailingly polite and channelling some of my previous retail experience (five years of working in running shops – if you have any running related questions please do just get in touch!) keeps the tone respectful and positive.

- 'I am really grateful for your support, thank you.'
- 'Thank you so much for your time.'
- 'Please keep in touch and just send me an email if I can support your child in any way.'

We want Jimmy's parents to be bemused about why he could possibly want to misbehave in our lessons, and presenting ourselves in this way can help. In fact, channelling some of the interpersonal and communication guidance in this book will help to present the best version of ourselves to parents as well as teenagers.

FLEXIBILITY

While there has been a repeated focus on consistency in this section of the book, one of the challenges of managing classroom behaviour is that we also need to have some degree of flexibility. While that may sound contradictory, it is ultimately about knowing who the individuals are who contribute to your class dynamic. Teenagers are remarkably complex, and we will quickly find out that what works to support one will not work for another, and that we will need to vary our style and communication with different individuals throughout the day.

Michael Marland, again, writes excellently on this issue:

> 'When all is said and done, however, you will have to vary your approach to suit the individuals you teach. You must be consistent from occasion to occasion, but flexible from individual to individual. One of the specialisms of a school is that of knowing pupils. You will subtly vary your approach to each as you get to know him or her.
>
> 'With one you will need to remain always light-hearted, with another quiet and personal. One may require a look, another a sharp remark. You will learn that some pupils react badly to public rebuke, some can't stand praise in public, others won't answer questions aloud however hard you press, whilst some will try to answer a question before you have even asked it. Many pupils behave acceptably but cannot resist subtly baiting to provoke. The teacher who knows these pupils intimately knows how to side-step the provocation, retain his dignity and authority, and maintain a warm relationship. All of this requires a great flexibility of approach to individuals.' (Marland, 1993)

This is why the start of the academic year needs to bring an exaggerated form of oneself in the classroom – to allow you the space to get to know the individuals and what behavioural cues they will respond to. While 'don't smile till Christmas' is indeed nonsense, we want to be firmer and obsessive about behaviour in the first few weeks with a class. This is why managing behaviour quietly is also so helpful: because it allows us to take this differentiated approach. The more obvious and confrontational we are in our environments, the more we open ourselves up to a lack of consistency in approach or fairness. This 'sidestepping' that Marland outlines is much easier to accomplish when we are approaching behaviour in this way.

Behaviour role models

It is worth concluding this section of the book by being somewhat circular. The cold reality is that teaching can be an utterly miserable job if you cannot manage a room of teenagers. Scripting responses and following the guidance in this section of the book will hopefully help in the mission to secure a positive environment.

The elusive question of 'how do I get better at managing my classroom?' is also supported by finding behaviour role models. I firmly believe that each school should identify the staff who manage behaviour effectively and encourage others to go and watch them. It could be several members of staff, all of whom model the different ways in which behaviour can be approached.

Even 10 minutes in another teacher's classroom with a focus on observing behaviour can be so helpful. Ignore content completely (going into a different subject area can help) and instead look only at behaviour. Watch how that teacher 'owns' the space – steal ideas that you can implement in your own context. Even better would be to have the opportunity to sit down and have a conversation with that teacher about how they got to the behavioural stage they are at – what have they focused on relentlessly?

This approach of watching others can also be enjoyable and energising, fuelling us with practical strategies to practise in our own classrooms. The best CPD I have ever had is watching and learning from the amazing teachers around me. Those amazing teachers also have the capacity to make two other complex areas of teaching appear seamless: managing classroom discussions and explanations.

Part three summary: script and teach behaviour

- Poor behaviour has the ability to destroy both learning and teacher morale.
- The reasons for misbehaviour can be numerous, including the complex impact of life experience, peer validation and simple boredom.
- There is vital preparation required before a lesson begins: establishing the environment and seating plan, planning an effective lesson, being clear on what may result in behavioural trigger points, and getting in a calm and confident zone.
- The openings of lessons are vital: positive, calm and with productive activity planned immediately.
- Outlining the purpose of any learning experience for teenagers is important, as is articulating the reason behind tasks and the structure as you progress through the lessons.
- Language used to manage behaviour should be polite (endless instances of 'thank you'), emotionally detached and clear. Diffusing potential conflict and avoiding hostility should be our aim as the adult in the room.
- Considering our positivity ratio is important in establishing effective learning climates: is our ratio more positive than negative? This means teenagers are clear on what the best choices are.
- Sanctions are important, but prioritise relationships. Make sure that when sanctions are used, they are used in stages and ruthlessly followed up.
- Parents can be a vital support network, but plan out and think carefully about how you deliver messages.

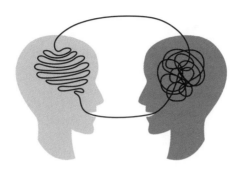

PART FOUR

LEAP IN CLASSROOM DISCUSSION

'There is no pleasure to me without communication: there is not so much as a sprightly thought comes into my mind that it does not grieve me to have produced alone, and that I have no one to tell it to.'

Michel de Montaigne (French philosopher and writer, 1533–1592)

TEEN TALK

What can a teacher say and do that will improve explanations in a classroom?

'Simplify phrasing but don't oversimplify it.'

'Explain with diagrams and giving definitions.'

'Be clear and use similes to explain what you are trying to teach.'

'Add videos to watch in your own time to recap things in your own time and at your own speed and make flash cards either digital or physical.'

'Speak clearly and listen to students if they don't understand and try to explain it in a different way.'

'Explanations are most successful when comparisons, diagrams and videos are used as well as verbal explanations.'

'Whatever you say, someone won't listen, so just be prepared to repeat.'

'Don't make it wordy, keep it slow and maybe do some tasks that involve students looking up meanings/explanations and write it down so they're more engaged.'

'Always make sure to explain as if trying to talk to a rather well-educated bird. Please do not talk down to those asking for clarification. Some students not trying to pay attention initially does not mean all students in need of a re-explanation or further clarification are inherently evil little goblins trying to destroy the lesson structure. It's normal to need exposition. There's a whole song about it.'

'Teachers should upload files containing their lessons/explanations onto suitable software (e.g. Teams). Also, they should avoid speaking too quickly or too slowly, and should speak at a reasonable volume. Use of OneNote can be transferred straight to our iPads when teachers draw/type on them giving us a direct experience. We need access to lessons at all times in case we need to check up on something. Teachers should avoid saying "you should've listened" or "why did you not listen?" as this gives a bad look.'

'Be thoughtful and say it with purpose.'

'Take their time. Also, come over to each table and see if they need help.'

'It seems simple but actively engaging with students is so important. I personally found I didn't pay attention when teachers put on a video or asked students to scroll through a website for an explanation. Asking us to engage in group/table discussions then calling on a random person in the group to ask what they thought encourages engagement.'

'Use criteria! I genuinely found that by having goals that were set at the beginning of the lesson – that would be completed by the end of the lesson – were the ones that I benefited from the most. Most kids don't use criteria, but by setting up a short-term goal that allows the kids to see what they have to complete, it helps improve so much in the classroom.'

'Involving the students with the lesson, whether that be experiments, acting, quizzes, games or even just having them read a part in a book. Anything that involves them is great because it encourages them to not just shut off their brains.'

'It depends on the subject, but the most general way is to show multiple methods of doing something, or explain it in multiple ways (visual, lingual, etc.). Most of all, leaving room for questions, and also asking intentional follow-up questions to students, is one of the best ways to explain things. There is a surprising number of people that I've encountered that won't ask any questions if they don't understand – a teacher might have to try to recognise these students and ask them questions to try to help.'

'Teachers could be consistent with uploading PowerPoints and make sure all information can be easily accessed for a given subject, perhaps even create audio recordings for lessons because teachers aren't always talking as per the PowerPoints and adding their own general and interesting facts, or hints for exams.'

'Apply the learning to actual examples. I had two maths teachers for one year. One barely let us take notes on the actual meanings and definitions and just did a ton of examples while the other had these long-winded explanations about meanings and names. I learned so much more from the first one as the questions were actually relevant for the exam while the second one was just unnecessary. Maybe that just applies to maths though.'

'Go round the classroom and ask individual people if they know what they're doing because some people don't like putting their hand up.'

'Analogies. Speaking in a language they understand, not literally, and making them understand by using things that might interest them. Get on the same level as them, don't talk down to them. It's more likely that they will feel bad about not understanding if you tower above them; it's intimidating. Use simple terms and define new terms.'

'Explain everything related to the topic from the very start. Like the processes that have led to what you are taking about. Include pictures and diagrams and link what you are talking about to something that the pupils already understand like a cultural reference e.g. in diffusion when a compound moves from levels of high to low concentration, you could also say that they want to go into a different area as the room they are in is too crowded and they don't have space to move around and play games. Additionally, answer questions no matter how stupid or basic they may seem.'

'Write what you are saying clearly! The teacher has to write down important key points in a class, not everything all messy and jumbled up, because remember, these aren't your notes. They are the notes for the students to take. If the notes don't make sense, how would you expect the students to be able to explain it back to you if needed?'

'I also think pupil participation is massively important in improving explanations – asking young people to repeat their understanding of a task, of a topic, encouraging group/class discussions regarding a topic, opening up the floor for questions, etc. Again, I think it's important to create an environment where there is no fear of asking for clarity on a topic. If a classroom is highlighted as a "safe space" from the beginning, it makes it easier for young people to ask for help or different explanations.'

IS DIALOGUE EFFICIENT OR EFFECTIVE IN CLASSROOMS?

The bedrock of any lesson in the secondary context is discussion. If we walked around any school with a stopwatch and measured the length of time classes spent in 'discussion' in its various guises, we would see it is a significant proportion of class activity. Often, however, this dialogue and time in lessons is not used as effectively as it could be. Perhaps on our stopwatch stroll, we see a teacher who is using their position to deliver what appears to be a sermon to a collection of apathetic and bored teenagers. Alternatively, we might stumble across a teacher who is initiating some kind of question-and-answer discussion. At surface level, it looks like an effective use of time, with some interesting responses to some probing questions.

We wait for 10 minutes, however, and see that it is the same three students who are answering every question. The rest of our teenage audience are either on their phones under the desks, asleep, or they have firmly switched off their cognitive lamps. The harsh reality is that often what constitutes good dialogue in a classroom is in fact a pretence, which not only leads to little learning, but actually serves to demotivate a number of students.

This communication section proposes a new way to approach dialogue in our classrooms. In the speed and responsiveness of the classroom, and in the midst of the cognitive demands on us, it can be difficult to think clearly. The acronym LEAP can be used to help us to remember to cover the essentials when undergoing any classroom discussion. It stands for: listen, explain, analyse, practise.

While this section will expand in detail on all four aspects, here is a brief overview.

Listen

One thing I know I have been guilty of in my teaching is to assume listening is happening – both in terms of my own capacity to listen and the ability of a classroom of teenagers to listen. That assumption takes place right at the start of the year when I believe that the class in front of me should be able to listen attentively. Clearly, to do so is both costly and wrong.

As this section of the book will demonstrate, listening is a skill that is under threat in our society. In our classrooms, if it is missing, there will be no learning whatsoever. It is why a clear and practical listening philosophy needs to be at the core of our classroom interactions.

Explain

It is a word that is deceptively simple, yet as we all know, tailoring our explanations for clarity and impact can be extremely challenging. The myriad of contrasting responses from the teenagers in the Teen Talk at the start of this section illustrate that understanding for them is deeply individualised – it can be hard to articulate what makes someone effective at explaining something. We will unpick various ways in which we can make our explanations more effective and efficient in this section of the book.

Analyse

How do we know if our explanation has been successful? Unfortunately, much of this is down to presumption in the secondary school context. We deliver a monologue that we think evokes breath-taking clarity, but really half of our class are completely bamboozled. It isn't enough to merely ask 'do you understand?' We need to analyse the response to the learning and explanation carefully.

The dictionary definition of analyse is particularly useful here:

1. Examine (something) methodically and in detail, typically in order to explain and interpret it.

For our purposes, it is about interpretation – can I move on? Are there enough students who clearly understand this before I can move to the next part of the lesson? How do I know?

Practise

Note that the final aspect of the discussion acronym is the verb 'practise', not the noun 'practice'. In its verb form it implies some aspect of doing – not something passive. It is a vital part of the process – whatever content or learning we have explained then needs to be practised by young people. They need to make sense of it on their own, through individual actions or through completing some sort of task based on it. If this aspect does not happen, the learning is often lost, and the discussion has no real value.

Let us leap forward into listening.

LEAP – LISTENING: ROLE MODELS

'The biggest communication problem is we do not listen to understand. We listen to reply.'

Stephen R Covey

'Why are you not listening?'

Listening in the secondary classroom is so often prefaced with negative connotations, giving teenagers the impression that to listen is some sort of chore. One of the central issues in this is that we forget that listening is a complex, multilayered process that requires explicit *teaching* in order to be successful. So why does this invisible art warrant a step of its own in exploring classroom dialogue?

Without listening, no communication can take place. To be more specific: without listening in a classroom, there is a complete breakdown in communication. Classroom teachers know this all too well – just consider how often we need to repeat ourselves on a daily basis. It can be exhausting and endless.

It is also true that the better we listen in our classrooms, the more we can encourage deep and profound thinking. Nancy Kline in her excellent *Time to Think: Listening to Ignite the Human Mind* highlights this:

> 'The quality of a person's attention determines the quality of other people's thinking.' (Kline, 1999)

This is particularly powerful if we consider that as teachers our role is indeed to 'ignite' quality thinking in classrooms. If we are attentive and attuned to our students, their capacity to think will deepen. Societally, we are also experiencing a listening vacuum – a void that teenagers arguably feel more keenly than any previous generation.

A missing skill

The *New York Times* journalist Kate Murphy believes that listening is a skill and art that is profoundly missing from modern society. Her book *You're Not Listening* makes this very clear:

> 'Listening is something you do or don't do every day. While you might take listening for granted, how well you listen, to whom and under what circumstances determines your life's course – for good or ill. And, more broadly, our collective listening, or the lack thereof, profoundly affects us politically, societally, and culturally.' (Murphy, 2020)

She goes on to use evolution to explain how integral listening is: we have the capacity to close our eyes, close our mouths, but no such 'off button' is applicable when it comes to our hearing. That strikes me as an interesting thing to illuminate in the classroom – it can show young people just how vital this part of them is, and highlights its role in helping them to learn.

The evolution of listening in schools is an interesting one. My 4-year-old is currently in nursery, and this notion of training listening is deeply embedded in everything they do. 'Listening ears' is a statement that he responds to instantly, placing his hands by his ears and giving complete attention.

There is, however, a presumption that by the time young people reach secondary school, listening skills don't need to be made explicit. Societally, that seems to me to be erroneous: listening becomes inordinately harder to do once young people reach their teenage years. Therefore, that notion of training for good listening should be just as, if not more, ubiquitous in secondary schools. And that doesn't mean berating young people and creating a negative culture in which we are forever criticising teenagers for poor listening. It means being proactive and teaching it.

Why it matters

We have already clarified that in the secondary classroom, distraction permeates at every level, and that teenagers' rapidly developing brains can add to the challenge of focusing. This is an issue because the listening that needs to take place in a classroom isn't passive; it is by necessity a hugely active one. Teenagers have to be attuned to not only the instructional guidance of a teacher, but also the deeper learning implications. There are also many other voices that require listening: most obviously in the feedback and discussions they will engage in with their peers.

Relationships are also deeply impacted by listening – and we have seen that the classroom is a space in which relationships matter profoundly. It is interesting to consider what happens when you ask someone what good listening is. Often, the answer relies on the negative – it is easier to illuminate what good listening isn't: fidgeting, looking around a room, interrupting, or lack of thought in the response.

Arguably this is because that is the kind of listening we experience on a daily basis – and it leaves us feeling underappreciated and ignored. We all have someone in our lives who doesn't listen to us well – they are distracted, they utter disingenuous statements, and they move the conversation instantly back to themselves when the opportunity arises. That in itself can cause significant frustration in trying to engage in dialogue, and can therefore potentially hold back the relationship.

Kate Murphy expands on this:

> 'Listening is a courtesy and, more fundamentally, a sign of respect… But listening is no easy task. Our magnificent brains race along faster than others can speak, making us easily distracted. We overestimate what we already know and, mired in our arrogance, remain unaware of all we misunderstand. We also fear that if we listen too carefully, we might discover that our thinking is flawed or that another person's emotions might be too much to bear. And so we retreat into our own heads, talk over one another, or reach for our phones.' (Murphy, 2020, p. 222–23)

Before unpicking this skill with the young people in our classrooms, we should start with ourselves: how do we model and improve our own listening skills in the classroom?

Teacher listening

We have clarified that teaching is one of the most interpersonally challenging of professions. That challenge isn't just about the extensive degree of talking we need to do; we are also tasked with demonstrating a deep and respectful manner of listening. A moment to reflect on the listening demands placed on teachers makes this clearer:

1. **Listening for behaviour**: making sure that the conditions in the classroom are conducive to learning.

2. **Listening to check for understanding**: can we be sure that the young people in the room are clear on what they need to do?

3. **Listening to peer dynamics**: as teachers we are constantly monitoring a room, checking to make sure the students' focus is on their work and checking there are no issues approaching that might derail learning.

4. **Listening to be responsive to questioning**: we ask a huge number of questions, which means we also need to have the capacity to listen and make sense of the information we hear back.

None of these listening skills are passive – they all require explicit effort. The effort, however, can have a huge impact in terms of what happens in our lessons.

Young people are, as we know too well, discerning: they understand when they are in the company of someone who cares and who is determined to listen to them. Adolescents are keen to engage with adults – even though it may often seem like they are trying to push teachers away, they want to have a positive relationship with us. They can also spot the converse a mile off: someone who is casting judgement on them, who appears disinterested in their ideas, who merely wants to switch the narrative back on to themselves as quickly as possible. To commit to improving our capacity to listen, therefore, will not only make us better teachers – it will make us better, more empathetic, human beings.

Mindset shifts

While we will look at more practical aspects of how to develop our ability to listen shortly, there is a fundamental mindset shift that needs to take place to enable good listening. It is one that seeks to view our classroom spaces as a place in which, alongside imparting information, part of our professional role is about listening deeply and with understanding.

I have been a volunteer for a few years with a mental health charity in Edinburgh called Health in Mind. Every couple of weeks I facilitate a peer support group for individuals with anxiety and/or depression. Now, I am by no means claiming to be an expert listener (just ask my wife!), but I do know that often my best listening of the week happens in those 90-minute sessions. Very early on, my philosophy was to make sure that people who attended the group felt recognised as individuals and validated. Often, that doesn't occur by seeking to provide a solution to how they are feeling, but to merely show them that they have been 'seen' and deeply listened to when they share. It is amazing how often this, in reality, is all people are looking for.

The minute we run into what the author Michael Stanier calls 'the Advice Monster', we run the risk of alienating individuals:

> 'We all have an Advice Monster. It is an embodiment of that desire we have to leap in and "add value" by offering a solution.' (Stanier, 2020)

Unsolicited advice happens so often, and with such frequency, that the recipients are often left frustrated: 'Here comes another totally biased piece of advice that doesn't speak to my context.'

Murphy suggests something similar in her book:

> 'Being aware of someone's troubles doesn't mean you need to fix them. People usually aren't looking for solutions from you anyway; they just want a sounding board… The best you can do is listen. Try to understand what the person is facing and appreciate how it feels.' (Murphy, 2020)

There is a 'way of being' that I have to emulate during my volunteer sessions: one that is receptive, without judgement, and very aware of the things that can stop me providing my full attention. I check in with myself regularly throughout the sessions, asking myself the simple question: are you present? That often means muting the inner monologue that can often be running while we attempt to listen to others. It means bringing that stillness, that connection and that curiosity that is the bedrock of deep listening.

How does that process work? Carl Rogers, the influential client-centred psychologist, called this process 'active listening', and said of it the following:

> 'I heed the words, the thoughts, the feeling tones, the personal meaning, even the meaning that is below the conscious intent of the speaker.' (Rogers, 1980)

The classroom is a different context, yes, but fundamentally that need to feel seen and validated is at the core of any group dynamic. For teenagers in the classroom, it is just as evident a need. That question also becomes very important when teaching: am I really present?

Physicality

It is so easy to get the physicality of listening completely wrong that it becomes something that causes irritation, rather than something that enables another individual to feel they can expand. Watch any expert listener and the first thing you will see is a stillness that is utterly focused on the individual. That stillness is balanced with sustained eye contact. As a rule of thumb, the listener should seek to hold eye contact more than the speaker. In the classroom this stillness and process of maintaining eye contact is challenging, given the opportunity for distraction around the room, but it is an important message we are sending to a class – when somebody speaks in this lesson, it is vital we all listen intently. Maintaining that stillness is balanced with open, encouraging body language. It is why not having our hands in our pockets or arms folded at the front of a room is important.

Leaning our bodies forward towards a listener can also help them feel ready to share more. A warm smile or a nod of the head can also help a speaker feel like they are being respected and listened to. The nod can be overdone – we just need to give the occasional movement of our heads to show that we are paying attention to a speaker.

Silence

To be a good listener requires us to become more accepting of silence. That, in a classroom setting, can often feel uncomfortable – and we often feel the need to jump in and finish sentences. Doing so, however, can be damaging to a young person's confidence and disrupts the messages we want to send in our classrooms about quality listening.

Silence is not only acceptable in the classroom, but it is a huge invitation for the teenager to expand and to reveal more. I know that the deepest insights and best answers in my classroom often come from times when I have deliberately muted myself, and given space for real thinking to take place.

Stephen Covey, in his book *The 7 Habits of Highly Successful People*, observes that 'most people do not listen with the intent to understand. They listen with the intent to reply.' That can often be the case in the classroom, with teachers conscious of the curriculum demands and the need to clarify thinking for young people. Silence can enable that focus on listening to understand.

Model curiosity

Listening and curiosity, for me, are also deeply connected. We want to listen deeply to something a young person offers us, because we are curious about what their unique perspective might bring. That is one of the joys of being an English teacher: having my own understanding about texts enriched and inspired with the original thinking that young people provide.

This can be supported with simple phrases:

- 'That is really interesting. How did you arrive at that thinking?'
- 'I'm fascinated. Talk me through how you got to that answer.'
- 'I love that. What made you think…'

Doing this not only helps to develop the metacognitive abilities of the teenagers in front of us, but it also assists in the building of warm and effusive relationships.

Clarify thinking

Part of listening in the classroom involves seeking to probe a young person's thinking, and to encourage them to voice some of that thinking. This can also be where we move on to asking some follow-up questions to really open up perspectives:

- 'Let me see if I am clear here...'
- 'Can I check to make sure I have understood you properly?'
- 'Can you expand on that?'
- 'Can you build on the detail there?'
- 'I think I heard you say ... is that correct?'

Summarise

One of our listening aims as teachers is to provide a point of reference and model how to summarise thinking for others. Once we have modelled this skill with a class, we can open it out and encourage others to do the same, so that everyone is listening intently.

- 'Let me see if I have understood you.'
- 'Am I right in thinking that you...'

This summary can also be tracked on the board as we write down the ideas that young people present during classroom discussions.

'What do you think?'

Sometimes we all need to feel like we have been noticed and that our opinion matters. I'm sure I am not the only one who has sat in a meeting brimming with thinking and ideas, but not feeling confident enough to share my thinking. The same is true in the classroom. Seeking out answers from individuals in our classes, with sensitivity and space for thinking, and then listening to what they have to say, can really help a young person discover their voice.

Henry David Thoreau (1908) encapsulates the sense of validation we need when we are asked our opinion particularly well: 'The greatest compliment that was ever paid me was when one asked me what I thought, and attended to my answer.' To do this is also to start to shatter the mantle of the teacher as the didactic expert. As we explored in the chapter on authenticity, to be an effective teacher you also need to reveal to young people that you don't know things and model humility in wanting to deepen your understanding.

The best teachers are continually reflecting and growing – they are lifelong learners. Nobody can know everything, so to continue learning from others is the best way to feel energised and inspired in a classroom. Being curious and seeking to find out what is happening in the minds of those we work with will really help to drive that forward.

To return to one of the books discussed earlier in the chapter – *You're Not Listening* – this capacity to listen intently in the classroom will also supercharge our ability to read the room and pick up on the nuances of understanding of young people:

> 'The best communicators, whether addressing a crowd or a single person, are people who have listened, and listened well, in the past and continue to listen in the moment. They are able to engage, entertain, and inspire because they first try to get a sense of their audience and then choose their material and style of delivery accordingly.
>
> 'And they also remain attuned to their audience while they are speaking, paying attention to verbal and nonverbal cues as well as the energy in the room to assess whether people are following them and care about the subject.' (Murphy, 2020)

If we want to influence the capacity of the teenagers in front of us to listen, we need to do so with integrity and through enacting that behaviour ourselves. Our capacity to actively listen and model good interpersonal skills will showcase to teenagers how to implement these behaviours. There are also other explicit strategies we can use to teach teenagers good listening skills.

LEAP – LISTENING: TEACH THE SKILLS

We have clarified that teenagers may often arrive in our rooms lacking the skills and awareness about how to listen. This – balanced with a lack of intentionality in planning and teaching effective listening – means that students often become non-reciprocal listeners. That, in short, means that they often adopt a passive role and don't offer any response or engagement with the information that is explored.

So, how do we make that process of valuing listening intentional?

Explain the 'why'

Like all communication in the classroom, we need to have a dialogue with teenagers about why listening is important, what it feels like and what it is. You could ask teenagers who the best listener in their lives is and discuss what makes that person the best at listening.

Other questions that might open up this discussion include:

- 'What does it mean to truly listen to someone?'
- 'How do you know that the person is truly listening to you?'
- 'How do you show that you are truly listening?'
- 'What are ways to convey that you are listening to someone?'
- 'How do you feel when someone doesn't listen to you?'

What this will hopefully open up is the understanding that when we listen, we learn – a core part of being in an educational setting. Then we can begin to take some practical steps to improve our listening skills.

Shut out distractions

I'm not sure if it is a sensory thing, but I can never teach with my classroom door open. It is like an invitation for the class to be absorbed by what is happening in the corridor: the sound of footsteps, the sounds drifting in from other classes, sounds of students being sent out in the corridor, and that provoker of all distractions – conflict. While closing the classroom door might not work in your context, the principle applies: make your classroom a space in which the young people's capacity to listen is supercharged and distractions are minimised.

In one of my previous books – *A Quiet Education* – author Joe Moran contributed a section about the value of quiet in the classroom – one that I would like to share again here:

> 'An English class could be, if nothing else, a break from the endless noise of the endlessly mediatised lives of young people – a brief respite from being constantly available to others via those familiar dancing thumbs on a touchscreen. It could be a replenishing pause – a space to stop, breathe and think.'

Following the guidance in the first part of this book will help with the way we present ourselves physically, influencing how simple it is to follow our instructions and listen to us. The next communication principle will also help to achieve this – by working on the clarity of our explanations, we ensure clarity in the following discussions and develop the quality of listening.

Direct attention

To listen well we need to understand what our focus should be. Far too often in the secondary context, teenagers' heads are bobbing between a teacher delivering information and a PowerPoint presentation. Now that many young people also have electronic devices in the classroom, this becomes even more challenging. Eyes and attention are diverted all over the place, and the quality of listening is low.

In planning a lesson, we need to think about what role other technology might play in encouraging listening. For example, a short, clear outline on a PowerPoint presentation can help to support understanding and direct attention in the classroom. Yet often there are several pieces of information employed alongside each other, which can easily distract students.

Simplicity, for me, is the key. If we want students to listen to us, we direct their attention to us; if we want them to read a PowerPoint, we direct their attention towards the PowerPoint. The clarity with which we direct their listening and attention to will support their ability to take in information.

Say it once

It is very easy to get in the habit of repeating instructions or explanations in the classroom over and over again. Doing so, however, is not only draining for us, but it also negatively impacts the quality of listening that takes place in the room. We know that laziness and our teenage audience can often go hand in hand: they know that if you are going to be on repeat all lesson they don't really have to pay attention. Instead, you can start instructions like this:

- 'I will be saying this once…'
- 'You will need to listen carefully as I will not be repeating this information…'

Once you have uttered that definitive introduction, it is vital you don't offer any repetition. At least some percentage of the class will have absorbed the instruction or information, so you can use them to ensure there is repetition of key concepts.

Some examples of how you might achieve that:

- 'I'm not sure I explained that very well. Can you repeat back what you have heard?'
- 'Can you clarify for us what we are doing next?'
- 'I can see you were listening beautifully. Can you explain what we need to do?'
- 'Can you just explain to me what you understand about the task?'

This can also be achieved as a pair task. Students in pairs have 30 seconds to check their understanding with each other about what has been discussed and to check their listening. You circulate around the room and listen carefully to conversations. You can then get two students who have done this very successfully to model this to the rest of the class.

One of the most challenging times to manage listening in a classroom is during whole-class discussion. Some teenagers will instantly see this as an invitation to switch off. A conversation about eye contact can help to make sure that they are showing interest in each other's responses.

Chart the conversation

Another interesting way to draw attention to pertinent points in a discussion is by using Doug Lemov's charting method:

'Charting is writing down shorthand versions of key points on the board during discussion. This keeps them alive.

'As the teacher, I can glance at the board and recall the gist of what Chris or Christina said. I can refer back to it, build off it, develop it. Students can do the same.

'It may sound simplistic, but one reason participants in large discussions don't build off – and refer to – one another's ideas is that they cannot remember them fully or retain them in short-term memory while thinking of their own idea. Charting helps overcome that and builds a strong incentive to respond to, and engage with, the ideas of others in the room.' (Lemov, 2018)

This charting process can also help young people develop their own ability to write down effective notes from a conversation. As mentioned earlier, it models quality listening and the ability to summarise.

Three questions

This technique is simple and easy to implement. During a discussion, or when listening demands are high, students can be encouraged to write down three questions the dialogue has opened up for them. This requires them to listen – increasing accountability – and to start to process the material that they are exploring.

Elevate listening

Positive reinforcement and returning to that notion of 'feeding' positive behaviours is a key message here. If we want listening to be valued in our classrooms, we need to showcase when it is done effectively. With younger secondary classes you can still get away with rewards for particularly impressive listeners: 'The Listening Legend of the Week' has got a particularly nice alliterative ring to it. There are also a few phrases that you can easily add to your repertoire to praise students for exhibiting excellent listening skills:

- 'There has been some brilliant listening done today, thank you, folks.'
- 'I love how much attention we are paying here, brilliant stuff.'
- 'You are focusing on me really well, thank you.'
- 'Thank you for some really strong examples of listening today.'

Now that we have secured the conditions for effective listening in the classroom – and have made its vital importance clear – we can begin to unpick what will help us to improve our capacity to deliver powerful explanations.

LEAP – EXPLAIN: THE COMPLEXITY OF EXPLANATIONS

'If you can't explain it simply, you don't understand it well enough.'

Albert Einstein

As a younger teacher, I would deliver an explanation to my students, confidently ask 'everyone OK with that?' and set the kids off to work. If I had a pound for every time that I was then faced with a thousand hands in the air from teenagers who had absolutely no idea what they were doing, I would be a very wealthy man indeed.

The process of explanation is the art of communication at its most deceptively simple: the attempt to transfer knowledge from one mind to another.

The complexity of explanations

The Collins English Dictionary definition fuels the idea that explaining is a simple process: 'If you give an explanation of something, you give details about it or describe it so that it can be understood.'

However, as those of us who have been faced with that classroom confusion know, explanations are one of the most complex acts of the classroom. To explain something to just one person can often be challenging (just consider the process of explaining directions) but to secure clarity in the minds of all the teenagers in a classroom is even more difficult. Thirty different individuals who need to glean an understanding from our explanations. Thirty different individuals who need something made clear in their minds, which was often previously unintelligible. Thirty individuals who bring a wide range of prior knowledge and prior life experience to whatever content we are trying to explain. We might think ourselves remarkably adept at explaining, but unless it has been understood by the recipients, our explanation will have fallen short.

And for our purposes, those 30 different individuals just happen to be teenagers. As we have seen, for all their strengths, some of them are not blessed with the attention skills that are needed to absorb explanations. In terms of our circle of influence, however, we cannot directly control what is happening inside the minds of our teenage audience (neither, thank goodness, can we jump into those!). It starts with us and our capacity to influence the teenagers in our classrooms.

To demystify

As an English teacher, I am fascinated by words, and my favourite synonym for 'explain' has to be 'demystify'. It captures the art of explaining well: from being confused and unclear, to having something opened up with clarity. Expert communicators in the classroom have invested hours in honing and improving their ability to explain things clearly to an audience. They can read a room remarkably well; they understand that they need to be hugely attuned to the young people in front of them. They rehearse, repeat and learn from hours of classroom mistakes in delivering explanations.

Sometimes these teachers are aware that in this complex process of demystifying, they need to model information – to actively show young people what it is they need them to do. They are also very aware that to explain something is a reciprocal process and that checking for understanding throughout the explanation is a nuanced process. They know how utterly futile it is to ask a room of teenagers 'does everyone understand?' These experts know that most teenagers will nod their heads vacantly in order to not draw attention to themselves.

These expert communicators are also deeply conscious of the fact that explaining has become all the more challenging in the modern era. Teenagers, like adults, have had their attention spans slowly eroded by the instant gratification of mobile phones and online technology. They don't, however, pointlessly complain about 'teenagers these days'. Instead, they take proactive steps to train the listening skills that were explored in the previous chapter.

This section of the LEAP acronym will examine the art of excellent explanations, and what better place to start than with our own subject knowledge.

LEAP – EXPLAIN: SUBJECT-KNOWLEDGE ENHANCEMENT

While we all have the capacity to pretend and act to a certain degree (politicians have this 'winging it' art particularly well honed), ultimately there can be no clarity in an explanation unless we are confident in our subject knowledge. Trying to explain something that we aren't completely clear on ourselves proves this theory – we flounder, struggle to find the words and often trail off.

In the classroom, that is a recipe for disaster.

If you ask young people what they value about a teacher in a secondary context, a large number will draw attention to subject knowledge. They appreciate being in the room with an expert who can enthuse them with their understanding of the subject. It isn't just that knowledge alone, however – it is the capacity to make that knowledge relatable and simple for them: to explain things with clarity. Einstein's maxim on explanations is particularly relevant here: **'If you can't explain it simply, you don't understand it well enough.'** So how do we arrive at that command of our subject that allows us to explain it with clarity?

Early career pressure

The pressure to fulfil that mantle of expertise can be very difficult in the early years of our career. Our individual subject areas are all immensely vast and complex. The simple fact is that we need to have a very strong grasp of the areas of our curriculum that we will be teaching in more detail.

Halfway through my NQT year, I was asked to take on a top set Year 11 class – all of whom seemed to either have more facial hair than me or were taller than me. They came not with behavioural issues, but with an intellectual arrogance that seemed to be deeply suspicious of my Highland simplicity (or so it initially appeared to my insecure mind – the reality was that they were absolutely brilliant and I look back on teaching them with very fond memories).

In the early days, I remember poring obsessively over my copy of *Macbeth*, trying to make sure I was crystal clear on every line – so when they asked yet again 'what on earth does this mean, Mr Thom?' I had at least some capacity to explain the information to them. The benefits in this process paid off though: the next time I taught *Macbeth* I was armed with a text that was annotated within an ounce of its life. I am also not the kind of person who can 'wing it'. I built up a high level of confidence through knowing that I had a very good sense of the material.

While we can 'act' our way through some things in the classroom, the capacity to mask a lack of subject knowledge is much more challenging. Teenagers know when we don't know our content, and they will ruthlessly punish us for it!

Subject-knowledge audit

Giving ourselves a kind of audit can help us check and develop our subject knowledge. Are we confident with every aspect of the specifications and what we need to know in order to teach the content effectively? This requires a degree of intellectual humility – surely, cry our degree-clutching minds, we should be able to walk through the content that we are presenting a 14-year-old with? As my adventures with *Macbeth* clarify, however, this is often not the case.

Sometimes actually completing an exam paper can be a very helpful way to break down any illusions we might have about how well we know our subject – I tried this with an A-level English literature paper and was shocked at the high standards. Once we have identified any holes in our knowledge, we can figure out how best to fix them.

Subject-specific CPD

Investing in ways to improve our subject knowledge will not only help the clarity of our explanations, but it will also help to motivate us further in our subjects. With the array of technology available to us now, there are so many different and energising ways we can do this. In recent years there has been an explosion of blogs, podcasts and books written by teachers that have one focus at heart: getting better at teaching and developing subject knowledge. For each subject there is also a huge range of other resources that can be used to support deepening subject knowledge.

Departmental meetings

The best departmental meetings I ever had were focused on what we were teaching and what we needed to know in order to teach it effectively. Learning from the experts around us and gleaning ideas from each other about how to approach the subject content can be hugely energising and inspiring.

If teaching was just telling young people what we know, our lives would be immeasurably easier. Not only do we need to be empowered by the content we are exploring with young people, but we also need to beware of the wonderfully hyperbolically named 'curse of knowledge'.

LEAP – EXPLAIN: THE CURSE OF KNOWLEDGE

'I know what I'm talking about – so by default everyone should understand me!'

We have all met people like this: whose vast array of knowledge is impressive, but they can find it hard to empathise with others when they struggle to connect with what is being explained. It happens to me whenever I have a conversation involving data or a spreadsheet (or, let's be honest, anything remotely mathematical). I just can't seem to glean any sort of understanding and manage to completely frustrate whoever it is that is trying to explain something to me.

That, in short, is the curse of knowledge.

In their article 'The Curse of Knowledge', authors Chip Heath and Dan Heath outline this in more detail:

> 'The problem is that once we know something—say, the melody of a song—we find it hard to imagine not knowing it. Our knowledge has "cursed" us. We have difficulty sharing it with others, because we can't readily re-create their state of mind.' (Heath and Heath, 2006)

In teaching, the curse of knowledge is ubiquitous, as highlighted in the excellent *Make it Stick*:

> 'Teachers often suffer this illusion – the calculus instructor who finds calculus so easy, that he/she can no longer place themselves in the shoes of the student who is just starting out and struggling with the subject.' (Brown, Roediger and McDaniel, 2014)

The investment in years of building expertise in our subjects means that we are expert learners. This niche focus is rewarded in a career like teaching: we get to spend our working days rambling on about the subjects that we love. That journey to expertise, however, can often mean that the various stumbling blocks that will have occurred are forgotten. In some cases, teachers have never had to go through that experience of really struggling in a subject. Often they have been very successful in their time in school. That means our explanations can be delivered on autopilot, without the real connection required to know what it is like to struggle to understand the subject.

Steven Pinker, in his excellent book *The Sense of Style: The Thinking Person's Guide to Writing in the 21st Century*, provides a good example of this: 'The better you know something, the less you remember about how hard it was to learn. The curse of knowledge is the single best explanation I know of why good people write bad prose.'

Having had the experience of struggling in a subject can really help in fostering empathy for learners. I know my own languishing in the bottom sets of maths classrooms has helped me immeasurably in connecting with all kinds of different learners, as has my complete inability to spell as a teenager (a fairly essential skill as an English teacher!).

Teenagers will not all share our effusive knowledge and passion for our subject: they will be, for the most part, novice learners. That means that the subject knowledge we need should also be combined with an understanding of the misconceptions that might exist in our subjects.

Avoid assumptions

'To assume makes an ass out of you and me.' What an important line for teachers to remember. Indeed, it is relevant in all aspects of interpersonal communication. Avoiding assumptions will ultimately improve our teaching, particularly as young people seem to have a magnificently sieve-like memory when it comes to understanding content. Just because you have taught a class one year of a particular age, there is absolutely no guarantee that the next year a similar class will understand it. The more familiar we are with the ability of a class, the easier it will be to tailor our explanations to their knowledge.

By rigorously questioning or testing young people on their prior knowledge, we can understand what we need to teach them next. Here are some ways this can be done:

- Fill out a brain dump (get them to write down all the knowledge they have about a topic).
- Do a low-stakes quiz (a short quiz on the topic that can be light-hearted).
- Test each other.

We need to be like a metaphorical hoover – hoovering up understanding from all our students to make sure we really understand what it is they know or don't know at each stage of the learning process.

Break down tasks

When we present and explain anything, we cannot jump into lecture mode – just because we are very confident in our knowledge doesn't mean that this will translate into the minds of the teenagers in front of us. Presenting material in smaller steps, breaking it down and checking at every stage that young people are following will help to make it clear. It will also allow us to pick up misconceptions at every stage of the process. This prevents us from launching into a monologue for a sustained period of time, then realising that we have lost half of the room during the process.

Always consider the literacy demands of your subject

With my English teacher hat on, this is often a rant that I feel leaves me frothing at the mouth and red in the face. Part of the curse of knowledge is the lack of consideration of the difficulties facing young people in accessing the literacy content of subjects. We cannot just presume that teenagers will understand the various subject-specific words that might work their way into explanations: we need to teach definitions and consider how we can increase understanding of them. More on that later!

Prior knowledge

One way we can avoid falling into the trap of assuming our students have a certain level of knowledge is to make sure that any new content we are exploring links back to prior knowledge. This helps to make knowledge stick.

> 'Whenever we begin to teach new content we need to work out how it connects to prior knowledge and explicitly make the links for the students. Thinking about foundational prior knowledge needed for a topic is a good exercise to undertake; "what do you already know that means that you understand this?" The more complex the concept the more foundational knowledge needed. This is particularly useful for trainee teachers. I've worked with highly intelligent trainees who struggle to understand why students don't "get" what they've taught them. Most of the time it's because they have the "curse of knowledge". (Cox, 2021)

So how can you test a student's prior knowledge? Short quizzes can help, such as a selection of questions on a PowerPoint presentation as they enter the classroom to test what they currently know. They can also formulate their own questions on a topic to see how much of it they are confident on.

Patience

We are all human, and there are a number of times when I have torn out hair in the classroom in frustration and been utterly perplexed how young people might not have grasped a particular concept – 'You genuinely need me to explain the difference between a simile and a metaphor again?' Yet one of the most underappreciated of teacher communication skills is having patience. We need to recognise that everyone in the classroom will develop understanding at a different pace and by different means.

Patience is a way of being that is explicit – you can sense when you are in the company of someone who is giving you space and time. In the public sphere of the classroom, it is even more evident, and creating a culture where young people of all personality dispositions can say, 'I'm still not sure, can you help me?' and receive help graciously is so important. So how can you develop more patience? It is a question I ask myself frequently as a parent of young children. It all begins by having patience with ourselves and not trying to force it by castigating ourselves whenever we do not display patient virtues. That in itself is counter-intuitive: patience starts with accepting ourselves. That sense of compassion and empathy is important, as is being able to recognise that all young people are different and will develop at a different pace.

The ability to take a deep breath, pause, and then persevere is the kind of attitude a teacher needs when approaching and explaining new content. A sense of humour and being able to admit mistakes is also useful: 'That was a terrible explanation, wasn't it!' This will be appreciated by teenagers and help them to see that we are also learning and developing.

Ask a teenager what will help them to remember content, however, and there is one answer that is always given: tell stories.

LEAP - EXPLAIN: STORIES

As an English teacher, I might bring a certain bias to this chapter, but I know what helps me to remember things is to package them as a story. One of the primary aims in explaining something to a group is to encourage retention – to ensure that they can go away and replicate it on their own. Looking at ways in which we can hook that knowledge for young people is very helpful.

What helps us to remember something? The simple solution often lies in telling stories. Cognitive psychologist Daniel T. Willingham suggests that stories are 'psychologically privileged' – that they can supercharge our ability to recall things. This clearly has an evolutionary basis to it: our ancestors used to gather round campfires and regale each other with stories, so it makes sense that when we hear stories now, we remember them more effectively. There are also some stories that are universal and that we will never forget: *Goldilocks and the Three Bears* is perhaps the most obvious example.

The Tortoise and the Hare

The reality is that most things can be presented in class as a story. As David Didau explains in *Making Kids Cleverer*, 'Almost everything we encounter we repackage as a story – scientific discoveries, news events, love affairs, the broad sweep of history. It is all grist to our mental story mills.' That requires some initial investment and planning from us as we search for something suitable and ask, 'What story can I structure this explanation around?' Once we have it, however, we have a resource that is rich and simple to reuse every time we approach that topic.

Any training I give on teacher wellbeing will always be packed around Aesop's fable, *The Tortoise and the Hare*, in which an arrogant hare challenges the slow, ponderous tortoise to a race. The hare falls asleep and the tortoise ambles to the win. It illuminates a message that to go slow and focus on sustaining ourselves can actually be much more meaningful and more powerful than anything else in the long term.

Education author and consultant Mary Myatt also writes about this:

> 'We need to take stories more seriously. Because stories are enjoyable, we have a tendency to underestimate their power. Great stories are important for their own sake. However, great stories can do some heavy lifting for us. Stories have the power to open up the imagination, to create the background for a new unit, to supply tier two and tier three vocabulary and to provide a context for the big ideas and concepts. They are one of the most efficient ways of providing a hinterland. Then stories contain sophisticated language of greater lexical depth and complexity than we would encounter in everyday classroom talk.' (Myatt, 2016)

Stories can also be very useful in terms of securing engagement and building curiosity in lessons, as students' interest is piqued in the topic.

Use your own experience

This is one that might depend on the teacher's disposition or on what they feel comfortable sharing. For me, this was always a rich way to teach personal writing that students need to complete in English. For a piece of reflective writing, I wrote and modelled a piece about a time that, very embarrassingly, all my clothes were stolen from a swimming pool locker. Students really enjoy that glimpse into our personal lives (and the thought of us being humiliated!).

While it is clearly easy to have that conversation with students in an English context, it can also be applied in other subjects. Often, bringing in practical experience illuminating how a part of the curriculum has been used in the teacher's own life can help it appear more useful and meaningful for the teenagers in the classroom.

Daniel T. Willingham, in his excellent neuroscience book *Why Don't Students Like School?*, outlines that emotional reactions to explanations will make them more memorable, but there are disclaimers too. We should be wary of a 'style over substance' performance. I like to use humour and often make jokes, but if your explanations turn into a comedy routine, you students will likely only remember the *style* and the jokes, forgetting the *substance* of what you are saying. Getting the balance right between engagement and imparting knowledge is a delicate process: making sure students enjoy their learning doesn't always translate to them remembering what you want them to learn.

Tap into students' stories

Teenagers have rich and exciting lives, often far more exciting than our own. I have been fortunate to teach in some very diverse inner-city schools in both London and Edinburgh, and that has always been one of the things I have loved most about teaching in those schools. Being curious and giving young people space to tell their own stories can help to strengthen relationships in a class and build empathetic awareness of teenagers. Once we know more about our students, we can ask them for their stories when they link to the curriculum.

Those students' stories then linger in the dusty recesses of our teacher minds, ready to be called upon at the right time. A story that begins with 'Billy, a student of mine last year...' is bound to pique interest in the classroom. It can then be used to showcase some particular strengths that helped that student to persevere through content.

Harry Fletcher-Wood, an excellent education writer, talks about how he uses a former student – Holly – to achieve this:

> 'Holly questioned everything. She wouldn't let an idea go, just kept asking and asking and asking, until she was satisfied it was understood. This process took time, but everyone benefited, because she made certain that things made sense to her before she let me, or the class, move on. Her determination to learn meant she always did, so she was wildly successful.' (Fletcher-Wood, 2016)

Holly's curiosity and intellectual perseverance makes her an excellent role model to share with a class. But there is a catch here: the rationale for telling the story needs to made very clear. We need teenagers not only to remember the interesting story we have told, but also to know the content behind it. That is why we need to have a range of strategies to check that the explanation has been understood by the teenagers in the classroom, which we will look at in the analyse section of our acronym.

LEAP – EXPLAIN: SIMPLIFY EXPLANATIONS

Let's look at another Einstein quotation, as it seems to encapsulate much of what is important and challenging about being a teacher and delivering explanations: 'Genius is making complex ideas simple, not making simple ideas complex.' Surely that means we can just send our intrepid teenagers to the dictionary to find out for themselves what something means? Or, given the ubiquity of electronic devices in classrooms, to look it up on their iPads? This, however, often creates more challenges and takes much longer than a decent explanation. Take the dictionary definition of osmosis as an example:

> 1. BIOLOGY•CHEMISTRY
>
> a process by which molecules of a solvent tend to pass through a semipermeable membrane from a less concentrated solution into a more concentrated one.
>
> the process of gradual or unconscious assimilation of ideas, knowledge, etc.
>
> 'by some strange political osmosis, private reputations became public'

Has that cleared things up for you? I thought not. So, now that we have clarified we are not about to be replaced by dictionaries or indeed Google, how do we make our explanations as simple as possible in the classroom?

Prioritise

In our position as experts, with passion and interest in our subjects, it can often be tempting to reveal every small detail of the aspect we are explaining. We have a (maybe) captivated audience to rant to about something that matters to us, so it can be tempting to share too much information. Instead of doing this, we need to break down exactly what we want to share in terms of the explanation. We need to keep out of the weeds of the explanation and instead consider exactly how much the students truly need to know. Thinking about the key vocabulary we are using will help with this intention: making sure we are keeping the language simple and focused, and only using the key words we want young people to retain. We should also reduce sentence length and increase the capacity we have to pause when delivering information.

Repetition

One way to improve our capacity to explain key terms is to use the power of repetition in the classroom. There is no doubt it can make content more memorable and easily accessible – just look at Obama's 'Yes We Can' speech.

If you make something simple then it is repeatable, and ultimately if you make something repeatable then it is understandable. Again, this requires some planning. We need to be clear on what the essential information is that we want to repeat with young people. Then we can be deliberate in terms of outlining it in our explanations and in the interactions we have with young people. We can then use questioning as we go around the room to ask young people to repeat content back to us to check understanding.

Curiosity

An explanation is much more likely to stick with teenagers if they are interested in the content and if the design of the lesson is such that they want to find out more. Considering ways in which you could generate curiosity can help:

- Is there a thought-provoking image, quotation or clip you could use to make things interesting before leading into more of the content?
- Is there a story that you can use to lead into the explanation?
- Humour always assists in building curiosity and interest: is there a way you could build this in to make it relevant?

Choral repetition

A nice way to make sure that an explanation lands with a class is to use choral repetition. This involves the class learning a new piece of content, such as the definition of a word, then repeating it back together to ensure that understanding is secured. In his excellent blog – teacherhead.com – Tom Sherrington writes about this:

> 'The quickest way to get everyone saying a word or phrase is all at once. Make choral repetition a natural everyday feature of lessons, say new words together, repeatedly. Then cold call a few students to check individual responses – this guards against individuals masking their half-hearted mumbles in the choral throng, not really practising.' (Sherrington, 2021)

Repeated exposure to new vocabulary

Alex Quigley, author of the *Closing the Gap* series, writes excellently on how to ensure that new vocabulary sticks with students:

> 'In most explanations there are one or two key words that you want to stick in the minds of students. In my year 10 English class I am currently comparing Shakespeare's 'Sonnets' with 'Romeo and Juliet'. Subject specific words that litter my explanations repeatedly include rhetorical terms like 'hyperbole' and 'oxymorons'. We have explored the etymology of those words, explored examples and repeatedly modelled them in our writing. With regular repetition such key words become the touchstones of effective explanations and we stress these words in our delivery for explicit emphasis.' (Quigley, 2013)

Model the explanation

The verbal explanation might need to be accompanied by some live modelling. In terms of securing information in the long-term memory, this helps to bring the material to life for teenagers. I always love watching science lessons in this regard, because the explanation is often excitingly and dynamically bought to life by an experiment that the young people get the chance to do. Providing some kind of model will help to illuminate further understanding of whatever we are teaching.

It might be that you model on the board a diagram or a paragraph while you teach the concept. So, if I was teaching analytical writing, I would model on the board what an analytical paragraph would look like, making sure that I check at each stage of the process that the young people have gained an understanding about what I have done and why.

LEAP – EXPLAIN: UNDERSTAND COGNITIVE LOAD THEORY

Dylan Wiliam tweeted on 26 January 2017 that he had 'come to the conclusion Sweller's Cognitive Load Theory is the single most important thing for teachers to know'. Google searches for 'what is Cognitive Load Theory' on that day must have exploded as perplexed teachers, desperate to be at the cutting edge of educational theory, sought clarity. In fact, that search turns up 48,100,100 results now, showing just how topical it is.

So, what is it, and what are its implications for how we structure explanations?

Definition

'Cognitive load' relates to the amount of information that can be held in our working memory at one time. John Sweller, who coined the term in 1988, said that since working memory has a limited capacity, instructional methods should avoid overloading it with additional activities that don't directly contribute to learning. This is what he has said about it:

> 'Cognitive load theory has been designed to provide guidelines intended to assist in the presentation of information in a manner that encourages learner activities that optimize intellectual performance. The theory assumes a limited capacity working memory that includes **partially independent subcomponents** to deal with auditory/verbal material and visual/2- or 3-dimensional information as well as an effectively unlimited long-term memory,

holding schemas that vary in their degree of automation. These structures and functions of human **cognitive architecture** have been used to design a variety of novel instructional procedures based on the assumption that **working memory load should be reduced** and schema construction encouraged.' (Sweller, van Merrienboer and Paas, 1998) [Emphasis added.]

To put this more simply: we need to be careful with what we ask the brain to do, because it can only hold a limited amount of information. The impact on us is that we need to think carefully about how we present new information to make sure we don't overload our students. In our aim to make our communication in the classroom more effective, this is vital. As Sweller identifies, 'The ultimate aim of cognitive load theory is to provide instructional effects leading to instructional recommendations' (Sweller, 2016).

There are three different forms of cognitive load. For clarity's sake, they are intrinsic load, extraneous load and germane load. Intrinsic cognitive load is the inherent difficulty of the topic itself; extraneous load relates to how the material is presented; and germane load is about the way the material is processed.

Here are some ways in which we can seek to reduce the cognitive load for our students.

Break up material

Any new material we introduce to students should be broken up and sequenced. That is why the planning process requires careful selection of material, so we are not including elements that detract from the central information we want students to retain. We have to avoid overwhelming students by introducing them to too much content at once. That is why the checking process we will explore later will be vital here. Keep it manageable!

Sharing the key takeaways with young people so that they aren't lost in the translation is also important. Nifty acronyms (such as LEAP!) can help with this.

Use worked examples

This form of modelling is very helpful to show young people how experts approach the type of problem that they will be asked to do independently. As Ollie Lovell (2020) highlights:

> 'In the CLT literature, worked examples are a form of instruction that sits between teacher modelling, and student independent practice, and extends the period of scaffolded learning.'

Reduce the split-attention effect

The title of 'the split-attention effect' is illuminating in itself: it occurs when we ask young people to give their attention to more than one source when learning. This switching between two sources will hamper the quality of their learning. To make sure that we are not splitting attention when delivering material to students, we need to ensure that we select the material we are going to use carefully. Those materials need to be aligned with any learning goals and success criteria that you might be using.

Again, PowerPoint as an instructional tool needs to be reflected upon carefully here. Are you narrating a lesson over complex slides that include extensive and challenging information? If so, you are likely to be splitting the attention of the class, with their eyes wandering back and forth as though they are watching a tennis match.

Once we have artfully explained the content and ensured that our teenage audience have a good grasp of it, we then need to move to our next step: analysing how well it has been received. That in itself is a key part of cognitive load – ensuring there has been enough time for young people to independently wrestle with the material.

LEAP – ANALYSE: ANALYSE UNDERSTANDING

'Any fool can know. The point is to understand.'

Albert Einstein

We have already explored why it is so important that we don't assume anything in our classroom contexts, and we have seen how quickly things can be forgotten. We can have absolutely no confidence that anyone has understood an explanation in our classrooms unless we are rigorous in checking their understanding of it. Much like all of the communication skills in this book, the capacity to ask a question at the right time and to check the understanding is vital. That is why whenever we are explaining a concept, we need to think of the bank of questions that we will ask to assess how well the students have remembered the information.

We must also consider how to differentiate the explanation. We may need to circulate the room and offer an alternative explanation to those students who really can't grasp the points we are trying to make.

The checking trap

There are a number of traps that I have fallen into over the years in my quest to make sure that my ramblings have been somehow absorbed by the eager teenage minds in front of me – and to make sure they haven't spent the previous five minutes wishing they were anywhere else in the world other than my room.

Trap: Hands Up

'Hands up if you can tell me exactly what I have been talking about.' Three eager hands raise majestically into the air and I pounce on Herbert – the effusive and wonderfully intelligent teenager whose presence in my classroom makes me feel like the world's greatest teacher – and he recounts my explanation.

Now, this will be a helpful process to a certain degree – Herbert will no doubt clear up the information for some people in the room with his incisive intellect. The problem is that I presume all the class have understood, set them off and then I am greeted by an array of confused questions.

Solution: hands down

Doug Lemov calls this technique 'Cold Call', but I find that slightly menacing. I know as a shy and quiet individual in my own time in school, I would have frozen on the spot if I had been the recipient of a Cold Call that was barked at me. However, I have seen Cold Calling employed with real sensitivity and understanding, giving teenagers plenty of time to think. Allowing hands down with time seems to me to be a fair balance. That could also be balanced with the opportunity to check with a partner in a Think-Pair-Share style. Two useful phrases are:

- 'I will be asking three different people to explain what we need to do next in 30 seconds. Can you mentally rehearse your answer please.'
- 'You have 30 seconds to check with your partner to make sure you understood that explanation. Then one of you will feed back.'

At this point I need to know the students: there is no point asking Gordon first – he has spent the last five minutes scratching his head and appearing to examine the strands of his hair (always a concerning one). I will start with some of the other students, and I will then go back to Gordon at the end of the discussion and make sure that he is absolutely clear about what I am expecting them to do.

Trap: 'Do you understand?'

This has to be at the top of the list of the most frequent, and most pointless, questions I ask in the classroom. It has many variations:

- 'Are we all OK with this, folks?'
- 'Do we all know what we need to do now?'
- 'Any questions?'

Most of these are met with earnest nods from teenagers who have perfected the art of earnest nods over their 10 years or so experience of education. They know the teacher is merely asking this question to feel good about themselves, and that it doesn't really ask anything of them – or clarify any real understanding.

Solution: 'What do you understand?'

A simple rephrase of the question can fix this problem – one that means that the onus is on the young person to vocalise their understanding: 'What do you understand?' Whatever they say back to us will either reveal that they understand and are clear on what they need to do or that we need to explain again to make it clearer for them.

Trap: 'Summarise what you have learned'

While this is clearly more effective than me asking 'does everyone understand?', this process can make it challenging to glean how much the class as a whole have understood. Yes, we can circulate and look over their shoulders to get a sense of what they are doing. Yes, we could take in 30 books and mark them at the end of a lesson. But there is a simple solution that will save some of our sanity and improve our work–life balance.

Solution 1: Mini-whiteboards

Using mini-whiteboards can be a really effective way to assess how every student in your class has responded to an explanation. Asking them to complete a summary in silence and then hold all the boards up can also highlight any misconceptions very quickly.

Solution 2: Explain it to your partner

I will confess that this is one of my ludicrously overused teaching techniques that often has teenagers groaning with frustration: 'explain it back'. In part, that repetition is used to make it a classroom routine, so that they know they are going to be tested on whatever content I have been rambling on about. If it is a content-heavy lesson, this can help to break up the huge amount of information that can dominate a classroom.

In terms of our goal to simplify classroom instructions and explanations, this should mean that young people have the capacity to explain the information back.

How do we know if the teenagers in our classroom know what we are talking about? We get them to explain it in pairs to each other in their own words. The true test of whether we have really understood something is whether we can repeat it back in our own words. Sometimes that can happen immediately, and at other times it can be at the start of the next lesson – just to check that they can retrieve that knowledge and are able to explain it.

In the classroom setting, this technique can be made fun: get them to number each other one and two, then dramatically reveal that it is number one that has to do the explaining. Number twos shouldn't then be left free – they should have to summarise some of the key explanations in the feedback afterwards. This process can be livened up by giving them a set amount of time, by providing some key subject-specific words they have to use on a PowerPoint presentation, and by giving them the opportunity to take turns explaining the concept to each other. We can lead into it with a variation on the following:

- 'I'm fairly confident I have explained that terribly – can you explain it to each other more effectively?'
- 'What exactly is a metaphor? I would like number ones to explain it to number twos in 40 seconds. You must use the word "comparison".'
- 'Two minutes to explain what we need to do to your partner: GO!'

Seek feedback

We have already pointed out in these pages that effective communication is all about the receiver, and we have seen how challenging it can be to be sure that we are communicating effectively. We often rely on feedback from external observers who might grace our classrooms once a year and have limited understanding of its context.

However, we have a classroom of thinking individuals in front of us every day, so using that opportunity to continually gain feedback from them can be very helpful in improving our capacity to explain (and in lots of other areas of our teaching). This could be done in many different ways, such as a simple Post-it note for feedback at the close of a lesson:

- 'What did you find helpful in today's lesson?'
- 'What can I do to explain things more effectively for you?'
- 'What helps you to understand things in a class?'

LEAP - PRACTISE: PRACTICE MAKES PERFECT

'Knowledge is of no value unless you put it into practice.'

Anton Chekhov

Now that students are listening attentively, we have explained with clarity and precision, and we have analysed the room to ensure that all the students have understood, we can initiate the practice part of the lesson. It is this part of the lesson that is often neglected at worst, or rushed at best, as we realise that we have five minutes till the bell and haven't asked our students to make sense of the content explored!

The importance of practice is clear when we consider that this is the phase of the lesson that requires students to actively demonstrate and apply the learning that has been discussed. This is integral for us to assess how well the teenager can translate the discussions into an outcome, and is therefore a true test of understanding.

If we consider any adult skill we have acquired (or failed to acquire), it has required practice. My torturous attempts to learn to drive at the age of 30 are among my most vivid recollections! The importance of this practice is also linked to our aims to build confidence and maturity in our learners. In the secondary context, it is particularly vital we are working hard to build up teenagers' ability to take responsibility for their learning, and this part of the LEAP process is designed to do this.

Benefits of practice

While practice is clearly practically important, there is also the sense of independence and self-confidence that we are trying to nurture in our students. We don't want any exploratory learning to be lost, floating around in the ceiling of our classroom. Instead, we want young people to feel a tangible sense of achievement: that through careful scaffolding, they have managed to demonstrate the skills and discussions explored in the lesson. By enacting their learning individually, their self-efficacy as learners is developed – and it is this true motivation that we will explore in our next section.

There is also the fact that it is challenging to sustain a lesson that is solely based on dialogue. We all need to have time to independently wrestle with material in any context we are in, otherwise any understanding is merely superficial or performative. This time it is necessary to refocus into a period of scaffolded quiet work, done in conditions that help young people to concentrate. If we ask teenagers to practise their work in a noisy and distracting atmosphere, it becomes very challenging for them to be disciplined enough to not be drawn into off-task behaviour (or indeed off-task thinking). We therefore need to validate why we are asking students to practise independently, and how it will help them to consolidate their learning. We can do this when we are clear about the conditions we want them to work in.

Sacred silence

In my book *A Quiet Education*, I wrote at length about the need to challenge the rhetoric around silence in the modern school, with the focus on 'sacred silence'. Silence shouldn't be used as a means of punishment ('Your behaviour is outrageous. I want you to work in silence for the next 30 minutes!'), but instead be perceived as something positive. While I don't suggest that lessons should be conducted in monk-style meditation, I do argue that young people's capacity to work in silence should be strengthened regularly.

I have found that explaining to students that silence is something that manifests kindness has worked well. By enabling silence in a room, we are allowing each other the space and time to concentrate fully. Some phrases you can use are:

- 'We will be working in silence for the next 15 minutes so that we can all focus.'

- 'I'm really looking forward to reading your work, so I'm going to ask you to work in silence.'
- 'Why is it important we work in silence for this part of the lesson?'
- 'I've asked you to explore some really challenging learning today, so let's see if you can make sense of it in silence.'

Set goals

Before students begin their independent practice, it is helpful for them to really engage with the process and set themselves some key goals to try to achieve. For me this is often related to literacy – I tend to ask the students to write one or two key literacy reminders on a Post-it note while they complete their writing. One of my aims as I circulate is to draw the students' attention to these.

Scaffolds

The independent practice part of a lesson should hopefully have been scaffolded clearly through the earlier parts of the acronym LEAP (you have encouraged deep listening, explained content clearly, and analysed how well it has been understood in the class). There are still a few more ways you can facilitate the teenagers' success, however, while they work independently.

1. Use PowerPoint

This is where PowerPoint can be very useful. You can have some key reminders or scaffolds on a PowerPoint slide while students work independently. This won't split their attention, as you are not introducing any new learning as they progress. It isn't the same as elaborate over-narration either, which will disrupt the atmosphere of silence in the room.

2. Circulate with intention

I have mentioned already that circulating the room in lessons is often valuable time that teachers can waste if they are not using that time correctly. While young people are working independently, we can get a real sense of how they are progressing. This can be the time to have quiet conversations that are supportive and that clarify learning. It all contributes to the feedback-rich classroom that has been a key aim throughout this book.

3. The power of the pause

If, from your purposeful circulation, it is clear that the individual practice is not going successfully, and that the same misconceptions are ubiquitous in the room, you can interject and issue some key teaching reminders from the front of the room:

- 'You are working beautifully, but I have noticed a couple of key points.'
- 'I'm really sorry to interrupt for a couple of minutes, but I would just like to clarify a couple of things…'

This interruption can be phrased in a really positive way, and can prevent hours' worth of feedback in books that you might need to give! It also saves you energy, as you don't have to make the same points 15 times as you walk around the room. The pauses can also help to initiate some reflective check-ins for young people to help them to evaluate their own learning and recognise when they are performing a task well or poorly. Again, some phrases you could use are:

- 'Are you following your plan?'
- 'How much time do you have to complete this task?'
- 'What do you need to do more of?'
- 'What skills are you using?'

Evaluation

A vital part of building our students' ability to take ownership of their learning is in enabling reflection and evaluation to take place at the end of an individual practice section of a lesson. Often young people will stop and enact some sort of pantomime collapse after a silent period of work, immediately forgetting about the work in front of them. Honing proofreading skills and running a critical eye over the work, however, will be vital training for them for when it comes to their final examinations.

Some questions that can support this process:

- 'What have I learned from completing this task?'
- 'What are my strengths? What did I do well?'
- 'Did I use my plan effectively?'

- 'What are my weaknesses? What do I need to prioritise doing next?'
- 'When could I use this kind of thinking again?'
- 'Does this represent my very best work? If not, what do I need to change?'

It is important that this process is also something that is celebratory. Teenagers are as inclined to experience negativity bias as we are as adults – and will often seek to find fault in their individual work. 'Here it is, sir, but it's rubbish' is such a common evaluation students offer when they hand in work. Asking them to identify their strengths, and making this explicit, can help them to feel confident.

There should also be the opportunity for the practice stage to be celebratory by asking students to share with the whole class or picking out excellent examples of work and sharing them. Asking their peers what the positives are in their answers also helps to make it really explicit what strong answers look like.

Our final communication aim is one that is integral to our success in the classroom: how can we build positive habits and motivate our classes?

Part four summary: LEAP in classroom discussion

- Classroom discussion is often time that is not used well in the secondary context, fuelling misbehaviour, a lack of focus, and a lack of learning.
- Using the LEAP acronym can help to make sure that this time is used more effectively.
- Modelling effective listening skills and an inquisitive and humble mindset will inspire deeper listening in our classes.
- We have to make the conversation about listening explicit: discuss with classes why it is important and remind them frequently of *how* to listen carefully.
- To explain effectively requires us to understand our subjects in-depth, but also to be aware of the curse of knowledge.
- Stories, analogies, and the pace and clarity of our speech all contribute to an effective explanation.

- Analysing how effectively an explanation has been received is important: using questioning, paired discussion and summary tasks are all core strategies to achieve this.

- Avoiding falling into the rhetorical question trap when analysing ('Have we all got this?') is key to really getting a sense of understanding in the room.

- All this dialogue and discussion has to be consolidated into some independent practice for teenagers. This helps their confidence and ability to develop.

- Discussion can be structured and scaffolded, but getting the right conditions in the room to ensure focus is vital.

—— PART FIVE ——

DRIVE MOTIVATION, BUILD HABITS

'We are what we repeatedly do. Excellence, therefore, is not an act, but a habit.'

Aristotle

TEEN TALK

What can teachers do to motivate you and build good habits?

'They can teach you how to do it instead of telling you the answer.'

'They should try to make their class exciting, stand up, skip around the classroom (not literally), randomly pick a student and ask questions about the lesson to keep everyone alert, because students get bored very easily if your class is like a prison warden talking to prisoners in a cold, damp, stone room.'

'Motivation is better when activities that the students find fun are incorporated into the work. It is also important that the possible career paths using the subject are explained in detail, giving the students an idea of what they are working towards.'

'Don't patronise me, don't tell me I'm doing amazing or great or excellent. Tell me how to improve. If I have nothing to improve, tell me what I can do next or even what I'm already doing well. Dull words and phrases to mark things I've spent hours on are unrewarding and disappointing.'

'Be more engaging or set a goal/reward so students will work harder to achieve the goal.'

'If you have already told a student to complete a task, and they are attempting this task, don't tell them to do it again when they are clearly trying, as it may dampen their mood and/or motivation. While 100% effort is preferable and should be praised, 10% effort is better than none at all.'

'Prizes, honestly. Might be costly but I've found classes more engaging. More games as well would be amazing. Not boring ones of course – stuff like Blooket as an example. Also, you should make the subject seem exciting rather than just repeating what the PowerPoint says and then giving us a task and we're done... We need enthusiastic teachers to make students feel excited to be in the class, and good, fun and unique ranges of tasks.'

'Be open and funny and make sure your students know you're there for them. Make cool presentations.'

'Be enthusiastic and make the classroom an enjoyable place to be.'

'Listening to me.'

'Have a countdown to the final exam once we know when it's happening.'

'Motivation usually improves with engagement and attitude of teacher. If I like the teacher, I will have greater motivation to do well in their class and engage with them as opposed to indifference. As such, being friendly to students (like saying "hello" in corridors or casually talking with them) will improve motivation.'

'Understand when kids may want a break or are sleepy. Don't point out every time a kid looks annoyed or bored unless you know they are OK with it. Personalise assignments for students because not all kids like making posters. Trust me.'

'I think it's important to have initiative, build a bond with the class. If somebody likes their teacher, they'll want to impress them, whether they know so or not.'

'There are so many students that aren't motivated by grades or promises that "this will help you in your future". Classroom games and competitions are some of the best ways to improve engagement, but motivation is something that I feel is ultimately a decision that a student makes for themselves. Whether they're going to strive to do well or procrastinate is up to them, and I don't think there's much a teacher could say without being redundant.'

'Be kind and helpful.'

'More interesting topics.'

'Make your classroom aesthetic and nice to be in so it'll put people in a good mood. Also base seating plans on who people actually work well with because some people might actually work better with friends around them because they feel they can't ask anyone else what to do.'

'Involve them. Give them a chance to say or do something related to the lesson. Reward them. Trust that they'll get it done. If they know that you trust them to do something, that itself will motivate them. Challenge them. Have timed quizzes or just games where you can test their knowledge and they can feel the buzz of competing.'

'There isn't really anything I can think of to help with motivation since some people (like me) don't have any, no matter what a person does or says, though you could take into account that a teacher could use words like "great job" or "nice one" if a person got something correct but they should refrain from using words such as "that is wrong" and instead use words like "this isn't entirely correct" and explain why! A teacher can't just say something is wrong and then go on to the next student for an answer. A teacher teaches, so a teacher should explain why an answer is wrong, but not really give out the answer.'

'I think it's important to highlight the efforts and achievements of young people. Even if it's something little, like offering an answer to a question for the first time, or if a young person attends a class after a long time – young people appreciate praise, and they deserve to be listened to.'

'Validation is a massive thing and can boost motivation. Being told you're doing OK, a teacher is impressed with your progress or proud of you can massively impact both the wellbeing of a pupil and their motivation and contribution. Just knowing someone is there for you and someone cares about what you do can be motivating in itself!'

DIY STRUGGLES

At the age of 36 I can publicly admit something that I have struggled through for years: I am utterly useless at DIY. Seeing as you asked, there is more: I can't stand it and will do anything possible to avoid doing it. It is a bone of contention in my marriage and with my father-in-law, who does most of the DIY-related tasks in the house.

How have I arrived at this point? In school, deep in the beautiful Highlands of Scotland, I had a subject called technology, which involved lots of woodwork. I was utterly terrible at it. I made a bird box that didn't open, got a pretty nasty and bloody injury from a saw, and was just a general disaster. When I was 14, the technology teacher gave me a 7 (the lowest mark) and wrote in the school report:

> 'While Jamie is a nice lad, I really hope we don't see him down in technology again.'

Although to say this stung would be an exaggeration of my emotional investment in technology, the 'really hope' seemed to speak to me of a desperation that I felt was a little unnecessary. Then began a long period of DIY avoidance. Many years later, my wife and I decided to buy our first house in Newcastle, which needed a huge amount of work. I attempted and failed to do many of the DIY tasks required. The project increased rapidly in costs, and my DIY self-efficacy dropped even further.

This very long-winded point makes something very clear: I very simply don't like doing DIY. I have absolutely no motivation for it. I have never managed to achieve any form of success in it; I have never had any clear guidance on it (or perhaps I should rephrase that: I have never shown any interest or receptiveness to receiving guidance); and I never received any clear feedback on how my skills might progress. The various setbacks

I have had on this DIY mission have secured my belief that I am simply incapable of doing it, and the best thing for me, and the world in general, would be for me to give it up. I have firmly convinced myself of my own narrative: that I am not going to be able to do DIY.

Self-efficacy

My DIY reflections are similar to how many teenagers may feel about our subjects, and they may have spent years feeling this way. They may dread going in, fixed in their perceptions that they don't like a subject and that they are terrible at it. Their fragile egos may have absorbed repeatedly negative messaging about their capacity to succeed in the subject so that, ultimately, they stop trying. Unfortunately for them, they can't merely stop – they have to attend our subjects until they are in a position to drop them.

That, as we all know too well, is a mindset that is hard to fix. We are all driven to some degree or another by our innate beliefs and how we perceive ourselves, and self-efficacy and learning are deeply interlinked.

Judgement

The other – more concerning – reality is that if a young person has spent 10 years struggling through a subject and not achieving any sort of motivation whatsoever by the time they arrive in secondary school, then something has gone wrong during their education. As a profession, we are quick to judge and encapsulate teenagers with phrases like 'they just aren't very motivated'. The converse is also true – we talk about young people who try hard in our lessons positively and effusively: 'They are so motivated. They work so hard.'

And yes, some may show all the signs of a lack of motivation in our classrooms. They might need frequent reminders to focus and they might struggle to complete tasks independently. We might struggle to form positive relationships with them as they reveal an apathy and dislike towards us and the learning process. But that shouldn't signal acceptance and a label as being unmotivated for the rest of that teenager's experience in school. We can't afford to merely label a teenager and then not seek to inspire some motivation in them – to do so would be to let down that young person and allow the cycle of apathy towards learning to continue.

The complexity of motivation

The reality is that they are likely to be motivated in other areas of their life. Motivation is a complex process that varies according to each individual. Personally, I dreaded a great deal of subjects in my school days, but absolutely loved going to English and history. It was definitely a narrow range, but I was fully motivated to put all my effort into doing very well in those subjects. Building habits and motivating ourselves can often be very challenging, and it is of course even more challenging to consider it a professional imperative to strive to motivate all of our students.

But that effort will pay dividends. Those of us who have spent many hours in classrooms know how much motivation means: it results in more effort, increased attention, increased perseverance and autonomy. The opposite of these qualities that are revealed when a young person isn't motivated are harmful not only to their own learning and understanding, but to the progress of a class as a whole.

Habits also matter deeply because they can be developed to establish behavioural norms. They can also be significant in terms of saving teachers emotional and physical energy and in creating a strong classroom culture. This brings us to the final section of the book: how can we talk to teenagers to motivate them? What can we do to facilitate building sustainable and influential habits with teenagers? In order to unpick this, we need to gain some sense of what motivation actually is.

WHAT IS MOTIVATION?

Motivation is an internal process that impacts our behaviours. The word 'internal' is very important here – it means it is completely invisible and difficult for teachers to discern. We can see how motivated a young person is by how they engage in our classrooms, but often the reasons for them not expressing inner drive and motivation are less clear.

Peps Mccrea writes about motivation in his excellent book *Motivated Teaching*:

> 'When faced with competing opportunities, our pupils must have some way of determining where to allocate their limited attention. This is where motivation comes in. Motivation is the mental system that sifts through the opportunities available to us and determines what we should attend to.' (Mccrea, 2020)

For Mccrea, it is to do with the economy of attention – what teenagers are being encouraged to focus on and how. There are all kinds of different theories of motivation, so for the purposes of our work with teenagers, we will look in brief at a few before going on to consider what we can do in the classroom.

Maslow's hierarchy of needs

Maslow's hierarchy of needs is a theory of human motivation that proposes different levels of needs, arranged in a hierarchical pyramid structure. For us in schools, this means that before we can begin to reflect on how we support the cognitive needs of our students, we need to fulfil the psychological needs.

Maslow's hierarchy of needs

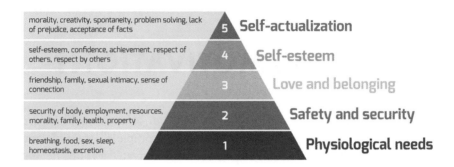

We need to consider the extent to which our classroom is a safe and secure place where teenagers feel like they belong. We then need to consider how we are nurturing their self-esteem, so we can help enable them to achieve their full potential and self-actualisation. Much of the discussion in this book has underpinned these needs, fuelled by a desire to understand our teenage audiences, provide safe and secure environments for them and to allow them to achieve success in our lessons.

Drive-reduction theory

This is another interesting theory of motivation that was developed by Clark Hull in 1943. Drive-reduction theory argues that the reduction of drives is the primary force behind motivation. Drives in this context refer to a state of tension or arousal generated by biological or physiological needs. A drive is therefore something unpleasant and we seek to counter it.

'When survival is in jeopardy, the organism is in a state of need (when the biological requirements for survival are not being met) so the organism behaves in a fashion to reduce that need,' Hull explained (quoted in Shrestha, 2017).

Attribution theory

Attribution theory was first introduced in the 1970s by Bernard Weiner. According to attribution theory, it is normal for people to look for explanations or causes that can be attributed to their own success or failure. An assumption of attribution theory is that people will interpret their environment in such a way as to maintain a positive self-image. There are three main categories of attributes for explaining success or failure:

- Internal or external
- Stable or unstable
- Controllable or uncontrollable.

Weiner (1980) states: 'Causal attributions determine affective reactions to success and failure. For example, one is not likely to experience pride in success, or feelings of competence, when receiving an "A" from a teacher who gives only that grade, or when defeating a tennis player who always loses…On the other hand, an "A" from a teacher who gives few high grades or a victory over a highly rated tennis player following a great deal of practice generates great positive affect.'

Self-determination theory

The next theory of motivation I would like to introduce was first coined by Edward Deci and Richard Ryan in their 1985 book *Self-Determination and Intrinsic Motivation in Human Behaviour*. Self-determination theory suggests that people can become self-determined when their needs for competence, connection and autonomy are fulfilled.

It relies on intrinsic motivation – engaging in activities for inherent satisfaction – rather than extrinsic motivation. The research suggests that individuals become happier when pursuing things that are intrinsically motivated – allowing them to focus on things they really want to do. Edward Deci and Richard Ryan (1985) define intrinsic motivation as 'the inherent tendency to seek out novelty and challenges, to extend and exercise one's capacities, to explore, to learn'.

What kind of motivation do we want to encourage?

Is there a common goal for us as teachers? In a utopian world we would arguably be striving for the following: they would be self-directed, self-motivated and, to use that wonderfully cheesy line, they would have 'a thirst for knowledge'. And we wouldn't want those qualities to manifest only in the short time we teach these teenagers. We would want our students to have an inquisitive nature that will sustain them for the rest of their lives: to become lifelong learners and autodidacts.

So, what can we do immediately in terms of our communication and behaviour in the classroom to influence how motivated our students are? Before we unpick that, let's look at some of the classic motivation mistakes we might have fallen into in the classroom.

MOTIVATION TRAPS

The Teen Talk at the start of this section reveals some fascinating thinking, but also highlights just how difficult motivation is to define and shows that we are all unique in what we look for in terms of motivation. Their reflections also explicitly highlight some of the ways teachers, with the very best of intentions, often try to motivate young people: the provision of chocolate; the 'reward' lessons in which nothing is achieved; the focus on engagement in lessons.

We have a degree of short-sightedness in what we believe motivates us and initiates the release of dopamine in the brain that comes from short-term fixes. We have clarified that long-term perspective isn't the strongest skill teenagers possess and that they are extremely sensitive to rewarding cues such as dopamine, so it makes sense that they value these above others.

And yes, these 'instant' motivational attempts might have some initial, quick-fix successes, but they don't provide the longevity we need in our classroom spaces. I have fallen into the chocolate trap often myself – 'Answer all 10 questions correctly and I will shower you in chocolate!' I also know how many times I tried and failed to make a lesson 'fun' in order to motivate young people.

'Fun' lessons

The time I tried to teach George Orwell's *Animal Farm* using hand puppets, for example, was very enjoyable for my class, but did absolutely nothing to support their understanding of the text (or my career prospects in that school when the headmaster decided to appear at the exact moment all of Year 7 were laughing uncontrollably and waving hand puppets around).

Daniel T. Willingham expands on this in his book:

> 'Almost every teacher I have met likes, at least on occasion, to start class with an attention grabber. … But attention grabbers may not always work. [A teacher] wore a toga to class on the first day she began a unit on ancient Rome. I am sure that got her students' attention. I am also sure it continued to get their attention – that is, to distract them – once the teacher was ready for them to think about something else.' (Willingham, 2010)

I am not advocating for deadly serious lessons. Of course fun has its place in the classroom – it just shouldn't be the default mechanism we use to try to motivate or inspire teenagers. The reality is that motivation in the classroom is much more complex and challenging to achieve than by merely handing out chocolate or dressing up. Any of us who have tried to build new habits or struggled to motivate ourselves to complete a project in the face of numerous demands know just how true this is.

There is also a fine line between engagement and motivation. I know, for example, that I am engaged when watching endless episodes of *Schitt's Creek* on Netflix, but there is no part of me that is feeling motivated. This is highlighted by David Didau and Nick Rose in *What Every Teacher Needs to Know about Psychology*:

> '[There is] a conflation between "engagement" and the motivation to learn. Much of what goes on in classrooms is predicated on the belief that if kids are sufficiently engaged in an activity, they will learn from it. But we can really enjoy something without learning a whole lot from it. For instance, many children will enjoy spending lessons watching cartoons, but they're unlikely to learn much curriculum content this way.' (Didau and Rose, 2016)

In terms of planning for learning, therefore, there might be some initial attention won from designing a lesson to deliberately 'engage' a group of teenagers. We need to carefully consider what we want students to take away and remember from that experience, however, and question if the engagement is taking away from the learning aims.

Praise

Showering our students with praise can feel like an easy motivational win and requires no additional planning whatsoever. Teenagers, however, are particularly sensitive to insincerity – and frequently throwing around words like 'fantastic', 'terrific' and 'outstanding' can demean the efforts of those students.

As Daniel T. Willingham writes:

> 'To motivate students – especially older students who are more discerning and better able to appreciate the differences between what is said and what is meant – teachers need to avoid praise that is not truthful … or has not been earned.' (Willingham, 2005)

Nick Rose, quoted in *What Does This Look Like in the Classroom?*, elaborates on this further:

> 'I think some of the arguments around trying to manipulate students' effort through praise and similar techniques tends not to work predictably because young people are socially aware. They have the benefit of a long evolutionary heritage of people trying to manipulate people. Very young children may willingly engage with the game in which they're manipulated to behave well, for instance, but as we get older, certainly when going through adolescence, we typically sense quite quickly when adults are trying to manipulate us; whether that's through rewards or through praise, and where they detect this, they will often reject these things.'

Specific and sincere

Motivating our students therefore requires sincere and specific praise. The sincerity comes from knowing the individual and recognising that they have invested significant effort or thinking in their response or work. That will, of course, vary significantly for each teenager, but it is ultimately what differentiation is all about.

In the praise we then offer, we don't just use a range of adjectives; we say what was particularly impressive about what they have offered. This makes it very clear for the individual what they need to replicate in the future:

- 'Well done. I like how you…'
- 'What is strong about that answer is…'
- 'I really like the way you…'

The motivational quotation or poster

Motivational quotations abound in this social media age – we probably come across scores every day. But do they have any real impact in changing our behaviour? I would argue that the likelihood is they don't.

If we cover our classroom walls in motivational quotations or posters, there will be some instant interest from a class and perhaps some initial discussion. Within days, however, it will become another blank space in the classroom, and within weeks they will be yellowing, frayed and ignored. It is better instead to manifest and model the values that are represented by these delightful quotations. Better to live them and make sure that any teenager who enters our space can visibly see our values and motivational qualities.

Exams

We often fall into using exams to encourage and drive our students towards caring about our subjects. The classic line is: 'You will need this in your exams in a few years' time.' Are teenagers really that motivated by the prospect of looming examinations? Perhaps when exams are immediately on the horizon they are 'motivational' but then it becomes more about using them as a necessity. This is arguably spectacularly overdone in the secondary environment. How frustrating if six years at a school becomes myopically about achievement in exams.

Ubiquitously making links to exam targets, grades and final exams actually causes more anxiety than inspiration for teenagers. As this section of the book will explore, the focus should be on the quality of the preparation and learning that will empower teenagers to feel confident for their exams. Let's start this exploration with how we can secure positive and motivational classroom cultures.

CLASSROOM CULTURE

We have already examined in this book how deeply teenagers are influenced by cultural norms and how quickly they seek feedback from their peers. We have seen from teenage feedback and research that this feeling can be almost all-consuming and profoundly influences behaviour. This isn't just limited to teenagers. Consider the culture of any workplace and you will see the influence of other people's behaviour and attitudes, and how quickly social norms are established.

Behavioural norms can be for the good or the bad. Seeing someone eat an unhealthy snack, for example, often influences us to seek out the same boost to our own sugar levels. To take a more positive example, it is also why people join clubs or groups. If you are keen on running, for example, joining a running club can be very motivational. You are, in that club environment, surrounded by like-minded people.

Groupthink is an interesting reflection of this ability to be influenced by those around us. It occurs when we are in a group and the goal to achieve a group consensus means we don't present any alternatives. Any of us who have ever felt uncomfortable about a group decision made in a meeting, but went against this intuition, will recognise why this often occurs.

Teenagers have enough school experience to be perceptive of teachers' ability to build a positive classroom culture. Some of the feedback I got from teenagers highlighted that it is clear from the start of a year what kind of teacher they have, which influences both behaviour and motivation for the rest of the year. Once a classroom culture has been established that shows the teacher to be limited in some way, it can be hard to win the group back. Those of us who have struggled with behaviour from the start of the year will understand just how challenging this can be!

So, for our purposes we need to consider how the best teachers achieve a positive classroom culture: how do we engender a collective mindset in young people that they can overcome obstacles and persevere?

As Peps Mccrea highlights again in *Motivated Teaching*:

> 'Norms play as big a role in school as they do in life, if not more so. They are the reason teachers can get 30 pupils to work diligently on sentence structure for an hour whilst some parents struggle for the same time to get one child to put on a sock.' (Mccrea, 2020)

One thing that we can profoundly influence to support the motivation of our students is the culture of our classroom. In doing that we need to be very explicit about what we want to see happen (normative messaging).

You belong

When I wrote a book about introverts in education, it was because I felt that too many young people were perceived as invisible by their teachers and that they drifted quietly through the school day without gaining the celebratory feedback or attention (for good or for bad) that their peers obtained. The same is true for quieter and more introverted teachers – when you feel your voice isn't heard in a school context it can be very challenging to feel motivated to be the best version of yourself. Not fitting in can lead to feeling ostracised and depressed. In order to support young people to feel that they belong, we too need to feel like we belong and model it.

I think this is a challenging part of being a secondary teacher: the sheer scope of young people that enter our classrooms on daily basis makes it difficult to build meaningful and individual relationships with every student. In order for them to belong, they need to feel like they are welcomed and celebrated in our space. But it is more than that: in order for them to not feel anxious or excluded in our classrooms, we need to be very conscious of our interactions with them. It is a central part of Maslow's hierarchy of needs.

What makes it even more challenging is the minority of students who often dominate a classroom. They might dominate for positive reasons – they have their hands up, they are bright and enthusiastic – or it might be more negative and relate to poor behaviour.

Goodenow and Grady (1993) define belonging in educational environments as:

> '... students' sense of being accepted, valued, included and encouraged by others (teacher and peers) in the academic classroom setting and of feeling oneself to be an important part of the life and activity of the class. More than simple perceived liking or warmth, it also involves support and respect for personal autonomy and for the student as an individual.'

Dr Kelly-Ann Allen (2019) has researched belonging in schools that corroborates this. She suggests:

> 'Building belonging in schools should be absorbed into ongoing practices that already occur throughout a typical school day rather than being an additional task. Starting with social and emotional competencies, and prioritising relationship and social skills, and emotional regulation can help lay solid foundations for a culture of belonging.'

1. Warmth and enthusiasm

It sounds simplistic, but we feel connected to people who manifest enthusiasm. We can embody this from the start of a lesson as we greet young people and discuss the learning that will take place. It is important that this doesn't sound insincere, and the phrases we use will be related to our temperament.

While the viral online clips of teachers who high five students as they enter a classroom might work for some, for most of us it is enough to use phrases like those listed below to express that warmth and interest in our students:

- 'Great to see you all.'
- 'I have been looking forward to this lesson...'
- 'I'm excited to have another excellent lesson with this class.'
- 'We've got some fantastic content to explore today. I'm so pleased to see you!'

2. Pronouns

We have explored how language relates to behaviour. It is useful to use pronouns in our interactions. All of this contributes to making the environment one of a team ethos.

If you consider any political speech, it is clear that pronouns dominate. A brief look at the final sentence of Barack Obama's 'Yes We Can' speech is illuminating:

> 'For when we have faced down impossible odds, when we've been told we're not ready or that we shouldn't try or that we can't, generations of Americans have responded with a simple creed that sums up the spirit of a people: Yes, we can.' (Obama, 2008)

In this sentence the pronoun 'we' is used six times. Personal pronouns have been staple features of political speeches since the dawn of time. But do we use them enough in our classrooms?

We need to build much more of this inclusive language into our whole-class interactions, and framing our language to include 'we' is perhaps the easiest way to achieve this. In doing so, we achieve three things:

- It builds a sense of commonality and rapport – 'We are all in this together.'
- It demonstrates solidarity between a teacher and a class.
- It is inspiring and motivational.

Some examples include:

- 'We don't behave like that in this classroom.'
- 'We are listening brilliantly, folks, well done.'
- 'This is challenging, but I'm really confident we can do it.'
- 'We have 10 minutes to do this task.'
- 'We will need to think really hard for this one.'
- 'We have worked so well, everyone, brilliant stuff.'

All of the above examples are useful for normalising effort and hard work too. That sense of collective optimism can go further as we encourage young people to see setbacks in their learning as opportunities for improvement rather than cementing low self-esteem. That positive reframing can become a class ethos again – one that young people might even begin to tentatively whisper to each other: 'Yes, we can!'

Young people are also often prone to elaborate catastrophising: 'I will never be able to do this!' Part of our role as teachers is to ask them to reconsider that with optimism – and 'yes, we (eventually) can' comes in handy here. We need to be the voice of calm reassurance, highlighting that all things take time and that all learning is a gradual process.

As Martin Seligman, the father of positive psychology, explains in his excellent book *Learned Optimism*, such phrases can be significant in engendering more perseverance in our young people:

> 'Success requires persistence, the ability to not give up in the face of failure. I believe that optimistic explanatory style is the key to persistence.'

3. Prioritising relationships

A culture of belonging in the classroom is also established by recognising just how important relationships are in the learning process. That is, of course, the student–teacher relationship, but it is also about how the rest of the class interact and show respect to each other. Modelling how we interact with each other in the classroom is an important part of creating a culture of belonging. Being respectful and calm, and modelling the listening skills explored earlier, will help build cultural norms in the classroom. A key influence in that is making sure that we are celebrating and recognising the diverse range of students in our classrooms.

To form those positive relationships, a teacher also needs to be able to inspire trust in their students.

TRUST

To spend hours in the company of someone every week can be challenging if you have no trust in them. Although there is much more to teaching than our personalities, being conscious of how we can create this trust is important. Trust is not a given in the classroom – as we all know very well, just being in the position of teacher is no guarantee that teenagers will do everything we ask. As we explored in the first section, some young people's relationships with adults are extremely complex and trust can be difficult to earn.

The Teen Talk throughout this book reveals how teenagers want to be 'seen' and 'valued' in the classroom. Trust works on so many different levels: trust in our subject knowledge; trust in valuing teenagers as individuals; and trust in having their best interests at the core. When that trust is present, the norms of the classroom are effective: the young people respond to what the teacher says without question.

How do we create that? Much of the dialogue in this book is important in securing trust: the way we present ourselves both verbally and non-verbally; the nature by which we manage behaviour in the classroom; and our passion, understanding and capacity to explain our subjects. There is also the fact that we need to behave with integrity and seek to model professional values.

Honesty

Although we have highlighted the importance of inspiring norms in the classroom, these all have to be based on sound ethical behaviour. If we are not honest with our students, they quickly work it out – and rightly begin to drift away from us. There is a temptation to believe that we need to appear as an all-knowing oracle in order to inspire faith in teenagers, but this isn't the case. They appreciate the strength that comes with saying 'I don't know' – after all, that honesty and openness is what we are also trying to encourage in them.

- 'I'm sorry, I will need to look into that – I don't know the answer.'
- 'Let me come back to you on that. I will look it up.'

A consistent persona that demonstrates an investment in the subject knowledge is much more likely to inspire confidence in a group of teenagers.

Empathy

Over a hundred years ago, Teddy Roosevelt uttered a statement that every teacher should be aware of: 'People don't care how much you know until they know how much you care.' That phrase has been manipulated in educational cycles and shouldn't be used to excuse inattention or misbehaviour from young people, but it is important to reflect on.

As teachers, we need to convey an emotional investment in our students to highlight that their development is profoundly important to us. The importance of individual recognition that has dominated this book is hugely relevant here. The interactions we have with young people must show that we are invested in them and care deeply. Phrases that can help to facilitate this include:

- 'I know this is difficult, but I'm really confident you can manage it.'
- 'I believe you can give this a really good go.'
- 'I know you have found this difficult in the past, but you have made so much progress recently.'
- 'I'm so proud of the effort you have shown in that task.'

Having secured a culture of effort and trust, we can look at ways in which we can support our students to build more motivation.

SET GOALS

In my work coaching teachers and leaders, I have come to recognise just how vital it is to set meaningful goals to motivate change – they help to frame the conversation and provide direction. Without goal setting, we are rudderless and aimless. By taking ownership of setting goals, we take control of our lives and development. Otherwise, we rely on others taking control of that process for us. Goals are vital in shaping our perceptions of work and what we do: someone who sets themselves goals will have a more positive outlook of successes and failures.

Breaking down goals

There is a caveat here – on their own, goals are not as helpful as we might perceive. It is fairly easy to set ourselves an enormously challenging goal. All we have to do, after all, is write it down or tell someone about it. That requires little effort and doesn't ask us to break the goal down into component parts, so we know what we have to work towards.

A few years ago, I set myself a goal. I wanted to run 10k in 33 minutes. Setting that initial goal took no time at all. The process that led to me eventually achieving that goal (thank you, Blyth 10k 2019!) was much more challenging. The miles and miles of running, the tracking of times, the different running sessions that I needed to put in – it took a huge amount of effort. The reality is that without the overall goal I wouldn't have had a sense of purpose, but breaking that goal down into manageable and achievable steps was what allowed me to accomplish it. That, for me, is why coaching is so powerful – because in the role of a coach, you are the one who holds that individual accountable and provides scaffolds to help them achieve their goal.

When working with teenagers, setting goals becomes even more important. There are so many different things competing for their attention, it becomes vital to structure some of their work and thinking for them in order to support them to achieve their goals. A great deal of interactions with teenagers involve chasing them to do things or applying pressure in order to achieve an outcome: encouraging them to set goals will help to prevent this. We have also seen how exerting too much pressure can cause significant strain on teenagers.

There are several helpful acronyms that break down the goal setting process for teenagers. ABC is a particularly ubiquitous example, which helps to give goals clarity:

A – achievable

B – believable

C – committed.

There are many other goal-orientated methods, such as employing the SMART acronym:

S – specific

M – measurable

A – attainable

R – realistic

T – time-bound.

So how can this help in the classroom? In order to feel motivated, students need to feel some sense of ownership over their learning. They need to recognise what their strengths are and understand what they are working towards. Choice, as we have seen, is also important for teenagers – they need to feel some sense of agency. By taking ownership of their goals, they are demonstrating choice and maturity.

Check-ins

Conversations with students about their learning are a vital form of feedback. These can happen during the lesson itself as we circulate.

During those individual check-ins, it is important to try to ensure that the teenager begins to take control over their progress in our subjects.

- Make a plan.
- Make it accountable.
- Include feedback.

Behavioural goals

Helping a student to take more ownership over their behaviour can be helped by setting clear goals that they receive feedback on. The language around that sort of conversation would be: 'Let's set some goals for you to work on regarding your behaviour. What do you think should be your priorities?' Once the young person has decided on a goal they want to work on, then it is helpful to break that goal up into manageable targets.

Returning to David Didau and Nick Rose's *What Every Teacher Needs to Know about Psychology* is helpful at this point. They ask a series of questions about goal setting:

- Are the goals too specific?
- Are the goals too challenging?
- Who sets the goals?
- Is the time horizon appropriate?
- How might goals influence risk taking?
- How might goals motivate unethical behaviour?
- Can goals be idiosyncratically tailored for individual abilities and circumstances while preserving fairness?

Goals have to be achieved in a way that is sustainable and manageable for all, balanced with being clear with young people about why we are asking them to do things.

ARTICULATE THE 'WHY'

'What's the point of this, miss?'

It is a question you hear dominating secondary classrooms across the UK: frustrated teenagers who cannot understand why they are being subjected to a lesson, for example, on Newton's Laws. This phrase is also ubiquitous because teenagers are notoriously difficult to motivate – and some will seek to question and undermine everything that happens in the classroom.

However, if we clearly stumble in our response – or arrogantly respond with 'it's on the specification, so you just need to get on with it' – we run the risk of alienating our teenage audience. After all, we all like to feel as if our time is being used well and that what we are investing time in is going to be meaningful for us.

Start with why

In his book *Start with Why*, Simon Sinek (2011) argues that very few people or companies can clearly articulate why they do what they do. 'This isn't about running a profitable company—that's a result. Why is all about your purpose. Why does your company exist? Why do you get out of bed in the morning? And why should anyone care?' These are interesting questions to consider when presenting teenagers with information. So, how do we begin to get them to appreciate the 'why' of our subjects?

Ten reasons

An interesting way to solidify this for ourselves as teachers is to complete our own 10-point plan. What are 10 reasons why our subject is vital for young people? This gives us some instant responses to the 'why do we need to study this?' conundrum. Every teacher of every subject should be able to rant passionately about why their subject is vitally important, and writing such a manifesto makes that thinking very clear.

Practical justification

Trying to find some practical justification for why you are exploring a particular subject area with a class helps. This can also be led by your students, helping them to make sense of a learning experience – in doing so it helps to avoid the eye-rolling that can often be a response to this question. 'How do you think this will help you in your life?' can be a useful question to ask.

- 'This will help you in your life because...'
- 'You will benefit from this because...'
- 'There are lots of ways you will be able to apply this...'
- 'Ten years in the future you will be using this when...'

Understanding of the world

Teenagers care deeply about the world around them – some of the most high-profile activists of the modern era are teenagers. The influence of social media has been hugely positive in this regard: they see what is happening in the world and engage widely with it. An understanding of the world impacts emotional growth. We can highlight how the time they are investing in learning will make teenagers kinder, more compassionate and more interesting.

One way to justify what we do in the classroom is to link it to the importance of developing an understanding of the world around them. As an English teacher this works well – the novel we are studying can teach them about the world in general and increase their understanding of a particular event or period of history, for example.

Making connections

Secondary school can often be a very disjointed experience for teenagers – they are marched to different, separate classroom environments without any real attempt to make a connection between the two. To help them make sense of that journey, we should make connections between the different subject areas. Those connections will help them to see that all aspects of their learning are interlinked, to persevere and to understand why they are studying it. There are several simple phrases we can use:

- 'This has a fascinating link to...'
- 'If you remember we explored a similar area last term...'
- 'Can anyone link this to any of your other subjects?'

Apply teaching to their experience

We need to encourage young people to see all aspects of learning as being integral to them (we don't, after all, need any reminders about how egotistical teenagers can be!). If students have an understanding of why they are doing things, it will help them to foster more resilience and perseverance, as they can see the value of doing those things. But perhaps the easiest way to encourage them to keep trying in our subjects is to give them a taste of something we all need for our self-efficacy and motivation: some success.

ACHIEVE SUCCESS

How do we support a teenager to excel in our subject and want to continually improve in it? Amy Chua, in the controversial *Battle Hymn of the Tiger Mother*, has some fascinating insights into how this might be achieved:

> 'What Chinese parents understand is that nothing is fun until you are good at it. To get good at anything you have to work, and children on their own never want to work, which is why it is crucial to override their preferences. This often requires fortitude on the part of the parents because the child will resist; things are always hard at the beginning, which is where Western parents tend to give up.
>
> 'But if done properly, the Chinese strategy produces a virtuous cycle. Tenacious practice, practice, practice is crucial for excellence; rote repetition is underrated in America. Once a child starts to excel at something – whether it's maths, piano, pitching or ballet – he gets praise, admiration and satisfaction. This builds confidence and makes the once not-fun activity fun. This in turn makes it easier for the child to work even more.' (Chua, 2012)

While some of the language here might not sit well with readers (Amy Chua also wrote in *Battle Hymn of the Tiger Mother*, 'The truth is I'm not good at enjoying life'), there is one core aspect of this that I feel is useful to reflect further on: the notion that excelling at something builds confidence and, in turn, motivation.

High success rates

Building a high success rate will build self-efficacy. This is applicable in any learning: the fact that my 4-year-old scores four goals at football practice on a Saturday morning means he will spend much more of the following week playing football in the garden and will in turn secure my future pension with a glittering football career. If we want teenagers to feel motivated and engaged in our subjects, we need to increase success in our classrooms. Those sincere moments of validation when they can visibly see their understanding and ability in a subject improve will achieve much more than a motivational quotation.

The challenge with this is that learning is often invisible and intangible. Metacognitive abilities are not hugely sophisticated in teenagers, so it can be very challenging for them to recognise that they are making progress. So how do we scaffold our lessons so that students are achieving success?

Lesson aims

One reason why the structure of a lesson is so important is because by providing clarity and a sense of routine, we can support the motivation of students and their ability to internally track their progress towards achieving an aim. That starts at the beginning of a lesson, by clarifying what the overarching aim is going to be (e.g. today we will be developing an understanding of osmosis). It would be even more useful to deconstruct that aim at the start of a lesson and explore together how that understanding could be developed, which could then be tracked as the lesson progresses:

- 'We are 20 minutes in. What have we achieved from our aim today?'
- 'How close are we to achieving the objective for today? How do you know?'
- 'Let's do a learning objective check-in...'

Sharing lesson aims at the start sets the class up with a way to measure success by the end of the lesson. Ideally all the young people in that lesson will be able to tell the teacher what osmosis is and why it is important as they leave the room. That gives them something tangible, and they can then run home and excitedly tell their parents what they have learned: 'Today we learned about osmosis!'

Success criteria

Another way to make success visible in a lesson is by having clear success criteria. This will ensure that the students are clear on how to take ownership of their progress. This can prevent confusion occurring when students are putting in extensive effort, but it is misdirected. They aren't clear enough on what they need to do to improve, and our feedback, combined with aims and success criteria, can open up that clarity for them and drive motivation.

Track your work

If things are going well in a classroom, there should be evidence of improvement over time. Of course, that isn't linear, and to expect so is to be overly simplistic. Although workbooks and jotters are slowly being replaced, one clear way to check a teenager's progress in a subject is to track that development in their workbook. In certain subjects this might be easier than others: in maths, for example, teenagers can clearly see what they have got right or wrong.

It can be a very positive way to use 10 minutes of a lesson: 'track your workbook and write what you have got better at.' This can then lead into a very useful classroom discussion, in which students explain as clearly as they can what they have been working on and how they have improved their skills. While this is beneficial for students' self-esteem, it also helps us to check their understanding of what they have in their workbooks.

The alternative is to have a fortnightly or monthly self-assessment that helps young people track the skills they have been working on. This can be done in a similar fashion to the above, with students outlining what improvements they have made over longer periods. A particularly inspiring teacher I observed asked her students to write to their parents or carers explaining what they had been doing in science that half-term. It struck me as a hugely positive way to share students' learning with home, while also celebrating the improvements they had made in science.

Balance

The focus on achieving success is challenging because we need the right balance of expectations in the classroom. If the work is too challenging, the teenagers will not persevere. If it is too easy, they will give up. To return to Daniel T. Willingham's points:

> 'We quickly evaluate how much mental work it will take to solve the problem. If it's too much or too little, we will stop working on the problem if we can. Working on problems that are of the right level of difficulty is rewarding, but working on problems that are too easy or too difficult is unpleasant.' (Willingham, 2010)

That leads us to our next discussion: how do we drive forward high expectations that will motivate students while also supporting them to achieve those targets?

COMMUNICATING HIGH EXPECTATIONS

One of the most obvious ways in which we can influence the dynamics of motivation in our classrooms is through the way we make our classroom expectations explicit. Language in this context is absolutely integral in establishing classroom culture and tone, and in driving aspiration and motivation. In the words of philosopher Ralph Waldo Emerson, 'We aim above the mark to hit the mark.'

We all like to think we can create an environment of high expectations in our lessons. To encourage the converse, clearly, is to do our students a significant disservice – none of us came into teaching to deliberately set low expectations. If we do find ourselves setting low expectations, the reality is that the young people will manifest those values and fail to push themselves to achieve all they possibly can. Yet how often do we really dissect what it means to *promote* high expectations? We presume there is clarity and directness in how we outline our expectations, but as we have already explored and as Edward De Bono (1999) highlights: 'useful communication must always be in the language of the receiver.'

Contrasting classrooms

The reality is that young people will come up, or down, to our expectations of them. The contrast in expectations can be glaring – young people may drift from one classroom where it is clear that aspiration is high, to one in which mediocrity in effort and behaviour are accepted. For the teacher in that second classroom, the vivid contrast between their lessons and lessons from the first teacher will make life all the more challenging for them. In terms of our dialogue on motivation, as soon as teenagers enter an environment that is perceptibly lax, unless they are remarkably mature and self-motivated, their effort levels will slip. Urgency and speed are part of this process – we need to quickly use our language to establish expectations as teenagers enter our classrooms, and we need to balance that with care and compassion.

It is true that curriculum will be integral to ensuring challenge for young people, as will cultural expectations in a school. But if that challenging curriculum is not delivered by the teacher with verve, passion, precision and direction, the students will not be able to make sense of the material.

Through our interactions with young people, we want them to develop self-efficacy and the capacity to persevere; that is why having a consistent set of messages is so vital to their improvement. We also have the ability to shatter confidence and motivation through our interactions – if we are too frank or too harsh in our feedback, this will hamper their levels of effort in our subjects. The research also tells us that the biases we think we might be hiding in our classroom settings are having a significant impact.

Our self-talk about students has to be optimistic and we have to believe in their potential. As much as we might try to outwardly manifest positivity and this culture of expectations, if we inwardly don't believe it, then we are going to struggle to fulfil it. The next few chapters will explore the phrases and words we can use (or indeed shouldn't use) to help to drive forward standards in our classrooms.

NO APOLOGY

'I'm sorry, so sorry
So sorry, so sorry
So sorry, so sorry
So sorry.'

REM, 'The Apologist'

Ah, the words that crush the spirit and motivation in any lesson – the apology for content: 'Sorry folks, I know this is a bit boring, but it's got to be done.'

It is said, of course, with good intentions: the desire to keep young people on side – a collective sense of 'we are in this (boring!) experience together and we can get through it'. It is another example, however, of just how triggering language can be. To utter such a statement is to negatively impact motivation in our lesson.

Considering our own social interactions can make this point clear. We have all met people who apologise before launching into a meticulously detailed story. We know what is to come will be fairly dull, but we are caught and unable to escape – trapped in their prolonged apology. As soon as we hear that 'sorry', our expectations are well and truly set – and nothing will alter them.

For teenagers, the apology has an even greater effect. Any student who was already struggling to find motivation in our classroom has now been handed a perfect excuse. The minute we apologise for what we have included in a lesson, we are permitting lethargy at best and inattentiveness at worst. We are also making a presumption that isn't grounded in evidence – for all we know, the class might find this topic utterly fascinating!

By apologising for the content, we are signalling that even we think the topic lacks interest or value. It will come as no surprise that the majority of teenagers I surveyed or interviewed for this book spoke of the vital nature of teacher enthusiasm and having an ability to spark interest in their students – and we need to think hard about how we will tap into that interest.

Of course, quietly, underneath our veneer of being celebrants for all things that we teach, we might just admit that we don't stay up at night reading about the difference between an adverb and a verb. To our unsuspecting teenage customers, however, everything needs to be presented as something that can add value to them and their experience – and that is intrinsically interesting.

Passion for content

Consider the success of public figures like Professor Brian Cox (whose success certainly isn't down to his illustrious pop career). In his television series, he radiates endless boyish enthusiasm and a real sense of passion for his subject. People want to spend an hour in his company; they want to experience some of that zest for knowledge and absorb some of it. He has spoken publicly about his approach to presenting and public speaking, and how it comes from practice:

> 'I'm not saying it's difficult, it's something a lot of people could do, but you have to be given the chance to learn, to practise and to grow. One of the main things for me was to forget there's a camera there and just allow yourself to be as enthusiastic as you would be in a lecture or a public talk.' (Brian Cox, quoted in Boffey, 2013)

In the secondary environment, this desire to be the recipients of enthusiasm and passion is just as keenly felt. Question teenagers on what they struggle with in a subject and they will often talk of boredom – boredom that can be associated with content or indeed the teacher. The huge up-take in science that correlated with Brian Cox's television shows, for example, shows just how receptive they are to that enthusiasm. 2012 saw a 36.1%

increase in the number of students doing GCSE science exams (Boffey, 2013). His show *Wonders of the Solar System* came out in 2010.

The resource that can help to alleviate the boredom that some teenagers experience in the classroom isn't a PowerPoint presentation or an iPad – it is how we manage to communicate a sense of excitement, curiosity and joy within our subjects.

Conveying enthusiasm

Arguably, the content that we know is less exciting has to be given a level of interest that is *more* pronounced, not less. The fact that our lessons are short helps on this level: if it isn't the most fascinating of subjects, it can be explored quickly.

The body language we discussed earlier also becomes important here. Given the reciprocal nature of the classroom, if we introduce new content in a dull and lifeless manner, our students will mirror that. Having a bank of phrases to introduce content with can heighten levels of interest and convey your own enthusiasm:

- 'We are going to be looking at something really fascinating today...'
- 'I'm confident that you will leave here today with some completely new knowledge.'
- 'You are going to want to share the information from this lesson with others...'
- 'This is going to add value to your life by...'
- 'This is going to be challenging, and I'm confident that...'

Instead of apologising for content, the next few chapters will give some ideas for how we can maintain optimism and engagement through our language. Let's begin by tackling the ubiquitous classroom phrase: 'I can't do this!'

TACKLING NEGATIVITY

'I will never be able to do this.'

Often teenagers present us with statements of permanence that include words related to time such as 'always', 'never' and 'forever'. They may then utter pervasive statements using words such as 'everything', 'nothing', 'everyone' and 'no one'. This is combined with linking everything back to themselves in their statements using personal pronouns. As teachers, the totally understandable trap we often fall into here is simply disagreeing with a young person: 'Of course you can do this.' This, however, is ultimately about as helpful as instructing someone to 'calm down' when they are feeling very wound up. It doesn't convince them they can achieve something; it merely adds to the internal frustration and stress they are feeling.

One of the techniques that teachers employ subconsciously on a daily basis, which is integral to generating a culture of high expectations, is reframing. Before we get to that, however, it is useful to reflect on the messaging that we do, or don't do, with a whole class.

Whole-class dialogue

In a class with particularly low self-esteem, a whole-class conversation about the mindset we bring to a subject can help to instigate more positivity. This is an example of when the anecdotes I shared earlier might help – for example, I often tell students I was convinced that I wouldn't pass maths.

Another way to increase positivity is to explain to your students that the words we use have enormous influence – when we label ourselves, other people or situations, we fix them. And to a certain extent, we fix our response to them too. If, for example, I call a new situation a 'problem', then my attitude to it is determined, because I've dealt with many other 'problems' successfully. But my attitude may well be very negative if I have only ever had bad experiences of dealing with problems.

Carol Dweck's work has a helpful simplicity to it that young people often gain in primary school: 'I need to apply a growth mindset'. Given how this is often used in primary schools, however, it has become a bit of a statement that is parroted at teachers, without any idea of what it means in practice. While this may resonate with 11-year-olds, it doesn't work to the same degree when employed by teenagers. It requires a more sophisticated and detailed approach to encourage perseverance with a task and overcome self-criticism and doubt. Trying to inspire this 'growth mindset' is clearly important, and we need to think about how we can do that.

Ask questions

Young people often overuse absolutes. We can challenge this by questioning them in a way that encourages them to reflect on these statements and reveals the narrowness of the their thinking:

- 'What stops you?'
- 'What would/might happen if you did?'

Both these questions force the students to focus on their barriers and elaborate on what is preventing them from either understanding a task or completing it. Once those barriers are clarified, then we can start to unpick them and provide a way to support the student.

Outcome thinking

When a young person presents you with a behaviour that's limited, unhelpful and unresourceful, you can help to reframe it by focusing on outcomes:

- 'What would you rather have?'
- 'How would you prefer to feel?'
- 'What will you be doing to make sure this happens?'
- 'Let's think of four things we can do right now to help.'

Both these approaches link to the goal setting that we explored earlier. When teenagers appear to demonstrate a complete lack of understanding by uttering 'I don't know', it can be just as challenging as when they use absolutes.

TACKLING 'I DON'T KNOW'

It is a phrase that teenagers appear delightfully familiar with – one that is usually coupled with a lifeless shrug of the shoulders: 'I don't know.' As we attempt to breach the small percentage of the class who volunteer an answer, we narrow in on an unsuspecting young person, whose panic and reluctance is instantly embodied in the phrase.

Now, unfortunately we cannot live by the classroom philosophy of Socrates: 'You don't know what you don't know.' To simply accept the 'I don't know' as it is first offered will influence the expectation levels in the room. If we do, there will be an unspoken agreement that highlights that not trying, not thinking, not at least attempting an answer will be accepted – and therefore achieving rigour and expectations will prove more challenging.

However, we also have the pace of our short lessons to reflect on alongside this. We need to be judicious and decide when to press individual students and when to move on. As we will explore, how we move on is also important in trying to sustain high expectations.

Sensitivity

Like all our interpersonal interactions in the classroom, the rejection of 'I don't know' has to be handled with sensitivity. 'What do you mean you don't know, you ignoramus! You are not fit to grace my classroom! Give me an answer now!' This is, of course, not particularly likely to lead to the light-bulb moment we were hoping to inspire.

The Teen Talk section mentioned the importance of patience, and we have looked at this already. In countering the 'I don't know' we need to first be understanding and give some space to allow them to wrestle with the ideas. Teenagers often hide their lack of understanding for many reasons.

If we respond harshly to someone who confesses to a lack of knowledge, we are not inspiring an atmosphere of transparency and openness.

Considering times when we have attended training as adults is a helpful reminder of some of the peer dynamics that happen in a classroom. For the minority blessed with confidence and high self-esteem this might not be the case, but for most of us it takes courage to volunteer an answer to a room of adults. Fear of being wrong, of being ridiculed, or of stumbling and revealing a complete lack of articulation are among some of the fears of adults. For teenagers this is exaggerated to a profound level. The unspoken laws around teenager dynamics haunt all classrooms, and self-esteem, as we have seen, is a much more fragile concept for teenagers. Therefore, the interpersonal safety that underpins the communication in this book is vital. The relationships we encourage will mean it is more likely that some young people will take part. Anything that serves to embarrass teenagers will breed a resentment that will make forming a positive relationship with them challenging. So how can we cajole them into volunteering some of their thinking?

1. Thinking time

Ideally, we want to pre-empt the 'I don't know' in our lessons or at least minimise its potential to take up time. One way to achieve this is to increase the time we give young people to formulate a verbal answer. By giving students time to discuss questions with their peers or to mentally rehearse an answer, we avoid putting young people on the spot. It provides a rehearsal space that is safe and stress free for those in our lessons.

Some phrases you can use include:

- 'Talk to the person next to you about this question for 30 seconds. How would you answer it?'
- 'Mentally rehearse how you might answer this question. I will be asking three people to share their thinking in one minute.'
- 'Use your mini-whiteboard to rehearse an answer in writing. How would you answer this question?'

2. Take a moment

All thinking takes time, and it may be that the young person is cognitively overwhelmed. Allowing them some space to consider and perhaps frame an answer in their mind will help to alleviate the pressure that they might feel. This can be done in a light-hearted and positive way that validates the fact that the young person is finding the question challenging. In my own subject this is quite easy. Highlighting that there might be different ways students can answer the question can be helpful to inject some calm.

You can also ask for silence to allow the whole class to reflect on their answer (coupled with 'I will also be asking one more person in the room'). Here are a few phrases you can use when a student says 'I don't know':

- 'No problem, take a moment to have a think and I will come back to you.'
- 'Let's all take a second to think about how we would answer the question.'
- 'It's a really difficult question; take a few seconds to reflect on it.'

3. Pressing

It is very easy to say 'I don't know', and when pressed the person can sometimes find an answer. My experience of coaching has reinforced this: the coachee will often try to switch responsibility to the coach, rather than take on the thinking themselves. An interesting response to this can be: 'If you did know, what would you say?' This encourages them to try to form a response:

- 'I think you might be able to think of something…'
- 'Can you think of anything that might help?'

4. Options

Of course, if your students say 'I don't know', sometimes they might genuinely be completely lost and need some scaffolding to provide the answer. If it is possible given the context of the question, providing them with two different verbal answers and asking them which they think is correct will be helpful. Another can be to ask for support from another young person in the room – like a phone-a-friend activity.

- 'If you did know, what might you say?'
- 'Which answer do you like best and why?'
- 'Which answer do you think is correct and why?'

- 'Phone a friend?'
- 'Fifty-fifty' – it could be this or this. Which is right and why?'

A final option is to move on to another young person in the room who is confident in the answer (using a hands-up approach here would work). The student who didn't know the answer, however, shouldn't be left to just relax. It is important to return to them to check they have listened and understood the answer.

- 'Who can help Joanne with the answer?'
- 'What did you think of that answer?'
- 'Was that right? If so, why?'

It is important to also consider how we ask questions in the first place. Are we open and curious in how we question the class, modelling the fact that there may be more than one answer? The more we show that we're looking to find an answer for what is inside our own heads, the more reluctant a young person might be to try to answer.

Within days of implementing the above techniques, young people will hesitate to utter a flippant 'I don't know', fully aware that you have an array of strategies that will result in them pouring out the answer to you within seconds. But what can we do when the answer is superficial or we feel that it doesn't quite illuminate students' potential?

Say more

While 'I don't know' attempts to curb any dialogue at all, what is a common recurrence in a lesson is an answer that is superficial. Again, it is entirely natural: often teenagers are trying to get away with saying the bare minimum. They try to placate our greedy need for depth of thinking by grunting a monosyllabic response to our challenging question.

While many of the strategies employed in the previous chapter will help with this, there are some other ways we can tackle this.

- 'Can you say more?'
- 'That's fine, but what else might you add to that?'
- 'You are on the right lines…'

- 'How did you get to that answer?'
- 'You are on the right track, but you are not there yet.'
- 'I can see where you are going but…'

Celebrate curiosity

The mindset of curiosity is one that constantly seeks to question and never accepts the first answer. It is this inquisitive mindset that we want our students to tap into. We can model that through discussions and our own enthusiasm for going 'deep' into our subject. Tangential discussions in this respect can be very helpful – they help to open up the numerous directions a discussion can take. Clearly, 'I don't know' is not something we can get away with as teachers, particularly when our students ask us for the feedback they need to help them improve.

FEEDBACK

Feedback is at the core of motivation and making developments. Unless you are exceptionally self-disciplined, it is hard to persevere in a task unless you receive some kind of feedback. Importantly, in a learning context, we are often fairly poor at estimating our current level of ability, so it becomes vital in terms of opening up clarity. As classroom teachers, the ability to understand feedback and how to apply it effectively is important. While we don't want to encourage young people to rely on external validation all of the time, considering how it might feel to be working very hard and never receiving any feedback or guidance on your efforts highlights just how frustrating being without it can be.

The feedback I received from teenagers was illuminating here: knowing that a teacher recognises how hard they are trying is a significant motivator. That quiet validation of an individual's efforts can often be more transformative than endlessly talking about grades and final exams.

Written feedback

Writing scores and scores of red ink on a young person's book is not going to inspire or motivate them. Neither will writing nothing at all, as it will show them that you have not read and reflected on their work. As any professional will know, feeling like you are being over-monitored can generate feelings of anxiety and stress, whereas feeling ignored means you search for validation.

There is also the challenging question for teachers about whether or not to grade work. Let's consider students that have just received the results of their practice exams. The well-meaning teacher has spent hours giving the students extensive feedback to help them for their final exam. They have also provided a grade. Immediately the students race through to the end of the paper in search of their grade. 'I got an A – get in! What did you get?' The classroom erupts into a mass of shared grade shouting. The extensive feedback goes entirely ignored.

Instead of this focus on performance grading, we want to explore the acquisition of skills towards mastery for our students as much as possible. When we receive written feedback, the thing we want more than anything is clarity – what exactly am I doing well? What exactly do I need to do to improve? Perhaps the most helpful feedback we can provide teenagers is clear, actionable and context-specific: something that signals to them exactly how to move forward in their learning.

Correlating feedback with a very specific goal or linking it to specific success criteria that relate to the task (as we discussed in an earlier chapter) can help to add to that clarity. The purpose of the feedback becomes about encouraging the student to persevere and work harder. This can be phrased in very clear and simple ways:

- 'What you have done well is…'
- 'Your next steps are…'

Ideally this process will happen as quickly as possible after the work has been produced. This will mean that it is fresh in the young person's memory and they can engage with the feedback received. To add motivation, encouraging a reflective self-feedback task can be helpful in furthering the young person's engagement. That could involve asking them to self-assess their work against the given criteria.

Responding

The notion of feedback being purposeful and actionable should empower the young person to respond to the guidance. This continues the dialogue and allows them to see how they are improving. The dialogue should always be focused on what they are doing and the teacher shouldn't be investing more time and effort in the work than the student. The student's response should then result in some feedback about steps that have been made to drive forward their abilities and increase their motivation.

Verbal feedback

Any time we are not engaged in explaining or instructing at the front of the room, the classroom should be a feedback-rich place. Phrases that can help support the impact of that include:

- 'How are you getting on? Can you explain how you got that answer?'
- 'What is going well with this task?'
- 'Can you explain why you just did that?'
- 'That is a really strong answer. How did you work that out?'

All of these questions help to make the thinking and steps that the young person is taking explicit, allowing them to talk through the learning in their minds.

We also need to reflect on who we are speaking to as we circulate around the room. The more extroverted students will be keen to elicit feedback from us, and the more challenging behavioural students will also take up lots of our time. We need to find all corners of the room and make sure we are giving space to have conversations with as many of our students as possible.

HABIT-FORMING

Two books that have sold astronomically in recent years are James Clear's *Atomic Habits* (over nine million) and BJ Fogg's *Tiny Habits* (over three million). The reason for their popularity is simple: we all want to forge positive behaviours that will help us to achieve our best in life.

Habit-forming, the theme of both books, is the process by which behaviours start to become automatic. Those habits can form unintentionally (like checking your phone a thousand times a day) or intentionally (I have a habit of drinking a pint of water when I wake up – and have done since I was about 13). Clearly, much of what has made up the content of this book has been with the goal of supporting teenagers to form positive habits. We have covered how we can seek to secure positive behaviour habits with them by scripting and proactively teaching behaviour. We have also evaluated how we might secure the habit of effective listening in our lessons, and how we can help teenagers to practise independently in effective conditions.

The above explorations have shown that if we can support young people to form good habits it will help them to save time when learning and building positive traits.

The challenge of habit change

The reality is that forming habits, or indeed changing habits, is remarkably difficult. We are all, to some extent, creatures of habit. As Charles Duhigg highlights in *The Power of Habit* (over five million copies sold), 'most of the choices we make each day may feel like the products of well-considered decision making, but they're not. They're habits.'

For most of us, the attempt to change a behaviour is too ambitious. A perfect example is any attempt to change our eating habits: we decide overnight that we are only going to eat superbly healthily. Most of us have also experienced the good intentions of a New Year's resolution rapidly vanish within the first 30 days of January. As James Clear highlights, however, such attempts to make instant change are unlikely to be successful. Instead, we need to break up the habit formation: 'If you're serious about making real change – in other words, if you're serious about doing things better than you are now – then you have to start small.'

BJ Fogg elaborates on this, by employing the metaphor of planting seeds:

> 'If you plant the right seed in the right spot, it will grow without further coaxing. I believe this is the best metaphor for creating habits.
>
> 'The "right seed" is the tiny behavior that you choose. The "right spot" is the sequencing — what it comes after. The "coaxing" part is amping up motivation, which I think has nothing to do with creating habits. In fact, focusing on motivation as the key to habits is exactly wrong.
>
> 'Let me be more explicit: If you pick the right small behavior and sequence it right, then you won't have to motivate yourself to have it grow. It will just happen naturally, like a good seed planted in a good spot.'

This strikes me as helpful when considering how we can influence habit building in our lessons: starting small and building from there. Our first step, however, is to include them in the discussion about how we can form positive habits.

Explore habits

If we are going to try to build positive habits in young people in our lessons, we need to explain how it is done. It isn't about manipulation; it is about them being part of this process. That conversation can introduce habit formation and explain how difficult it can be. I'm sure most teenagers can name habits that they have that are not the most beneficial! The conversation might even involve them suggesting and discussing what habits would be most beneficial in our subject and context, which may lead to conversations about the barriers they might face in trying to form those habits.

Getting them to fill out a habit progress report can be helpful in this context, clarifying for them what habits might prove useful in our subject.

Persistence

We have touched on this already, but building a habit that ensures teenagers don't give up is an important place to start. If we can secure that habit seed, we provide them with the tools to keep going in challenging circumstances in exams and beyond into their later lives.

Breaking down a task will help young people to persist with it, preventing it from becoming overwhelming for them. It can also help them see that if they continually apply effort, they are likely to improve. Doug Lemov writes about this in terms of encouraging writing in students:

> 'Start small and scale up. Ask for a minute the first time. Then a minute-and-a-half. Then two. Try to take the long view. The most important thing is to have students practice being successful at writing steadily through a block of time when asked to, not only because seeing themselves succeed convinces students that they can, but because it makes a habit of writing steadily through the time allotted whenever asked. The idea is that when you say go, they write straight through because they can't imagine anything else!' (Lemov, 2014)

We then need to make it explicit that they have achieved some success through their efforts, helping them to develop persistence. That helps them to connect their persistent behaviours with an intrinsic reward. Frequent repetition of the particular skill will also help them to develop persistence as it becomes a habit. We have already discussed the importance of young people understanding their 'success' in our lessons, and that is vital in building good habits.

Rewards

For any habit to form – such as a habit of coming into a lesson and starting effectively – there has to be some kind of reward. We have already established that throwing chocolate at teenagers for sitting down and taking off their jackets is not going to be successful. Instead, we need to frame it in terms of their progress in our subjects. They need to see that by quickly engaging in a lesson and starting a task, they are going to improve their ability to do well. That can come from our positive feedback or by encouraging them to track their work, to see how much quality work they manage to complete in lessons.

Habits are also formed through routines. Having successful routines that teenagers are comfortable and familiar with has been reflected throughout this book – particularly in the behaviour section. We want to make routines as simple as possible for our teenage audience to follow, so that they can form automatic habits.

Self-awareness in our teenage audience will also help them to form good habits. As much as we can scaffold things for them and design lesson activities and structures, we also need them to take ownership. On that note, a quotation from James Clear – 'Every action you take is a vote for the person you wish to become' – might well be a beneficial rallying cry to repeat with them, one that helps them see that they are ultimately in control of the habits they want to develop.

> ### Part five summary: drive motivation, build habits.
>
> - Some teenagers may enter our lessons deeply demotivated. Our role is to not accept this and to work hard to support perseverance in our subjects.
> - Avoiding instantly gratifying rewards like chocolate and the temptation to only teach 'fun' lessons will help us to plan for motivation over time.
> - The culture of our classroom is vital in securing motivation and norms. The culture should be one that provides security, trust and acceptance of mistakes.

- Helping teenagers to set goals in their own learning can develop their self-efficacy and understanding of how to move forward in our subjects.

- Teenagers need some sense of why they are learning things and how those things can support them in the future.

- If they can see how they are improving and achieving success in their work, they are likely to build positive habits and persistence.

- We set the tone for the expectations in our lessons: that means not apologising for content and not accepting 'I don't know'.

- Feedback is vital in supporting motivation and habit building, but that doesn't have to only be written. A verbal-feedback-rich classroom is going to be a motivated one.

- Habit formation requires routines, clarity and perseverance. We can support teenagers in forming these by explaining habit formation, scaffolding work, and helping them to see how they are making improvements.

THE INTERNAL COMMUNICATION

There has been a recurrent theme in this book: to communicate well with teenagers requires patience, compassion and a reflective mindset. These are, after all, the hallmarks of what makes a truly transformative teacher. None of these are easy. The range of students we deal with on a daily basis means that we are stretched interpersonally and it can be difficult to gain the space to offer solace and insight through our words.

To achieve that positive and empathetic external projection, however, we need to also feel that sense of positivity and calm internally. We all know how hard it is to take on the concerns of another person or project optimism if we are struggling internally.

The inner narrator

We need to tackle one dominant and pervasive voice that can at times seem to berate us more than lift us up and can feed frustration and perfectionism: the inner monologue.

Our inner voice follows us around all day, often offering an entirely subjective commentary on everything that is going on. It is one that can be very challenging to work alongside – much more so than many classes of teenagers! There is a reason why for thousands of years it has been referred to as the 'monkey mind' – it is the sense of it being entirely untameable and wreaking havoc.

Ethan Kross, in his book *Chatter: The Voice in Our Head and How to Harness It*, highlights the impact this inner voice can have on us all very well:

> 'However it manifests itself, when the inner voice runs amok and chatter takes the mental microphone, our mind not only torments but paralyzes us. It can also lead us to do things that sabotage us.'

Negativity

We have clarified that teaching is a profession in which perfection is unattainable. The constant flux and unpredictability of working with teenagers means that inevitably we undergo an emotional roller coaster just about every day. The evolutionary nature of our minds means we are much more likely to focus on negative reflections. Considering a day that was full of positives but had one negative piece of feedback from somebody can illuminate that well. What do we ruminate on obsessively that evening: is it the positive or the negative? For me, and I would imagine most of the readers, we focus on that negative piece of feedback.

To manifest positive qualities in the classroom, we need to treat ourselves kindly in the same way we expect and teach teenagers to. Although I appreciate in reality how challenging this is, we should actively try to recognise internally that making mistakes is part of life.

We also need to appreciate that negative internal thinking often serves very little purpose, leaving us frustrated and without enough energy left to think positively. Thousands of years ago, the Roman philosopher Seneca clearly recognised the importance of this process. He wrote: 'What progress, you ask, have I made? I have begun to be a friend to myself.'

As mentioned previously, in his book *Learned Optimism,* Martin Seligman provides guidance on how we can do this. He suggests we monitor the automatic thoughts and attitudes we experience and dispute the overarching pessimistic explanations that we can face.

> 'Success requires persistence, the ability to not give up in the face of failure. I believe that optimistic explanatory style is the key to persistence.'

Pause for the positives

An effective way to tackle our tendency for negative thought is to take the time to recognise the positive impact we have during our working days.

We ultimately need to make that process explicit – not many teenagers take the time to offer effusive feedback and praise at the end of each lesson. They will, however, feel it deeply if you take the time to give such feedback.

So how do we sustain a positive internal mindset? How can we fight back and maintain a sense of control over our inner narrator?

Gratitude practices

Positive psychology and gratitude go hand in hand. In the fast pace of life in school it can be difficult to find the time and energy in which to recognise what has gone well and what we have contributed to those more positive feelings. Gratitude practices can be very simple to apply. Writing down three things we are grateful for at the end of the day can help us to slow down enough to notice things that are positive in our lives. This doesn't have to be written. The last conversation I always have with my four-year-old before he goes to sleep every night is his 'Best Bits'. He lists what he has enjoyed the most throughout the day, and what he feels happy about. Channelling our inner four-year-old might feel a little awkward at first, but doing this practice will build a gratitude habit that makes us much more inclined to think positively.

Recognise our strengths

In her book *Positive Psychology in a Nutshell*, Ilona Boniwell argues that in order to achieve happiness and professional success, we need to be very clear on our strengths:

> 'Essentially top achievers build their personal lives and careers on their talents and strengths. They learn to recognise their talents and develop them further. They find the roles that suit them best and they invent ways to apply their talents and strengths in their lives. As far as weaknesses are concerned, they manage rather than develop them.'

Coaching and dialogue

Taking the time to have deep dialogue with colleagues and others can help to keep us positive internally. It can be very easy to get caught in our own internal projections of events and struggle to find a sense of both peace and clarity. Finding the people in our lives who are good listeners and can help us to work through issues really helps in this regard. While listening is important, we also need to be asked questions or given advice to help us at times re-evaluate a situation.

Perspective

Another way to maintain a healthy and positive perspective about events that take place is by asking yourself how you will feel about something in the future. At times we can let the immediacy of a stressful experience colour our perceptions, and we believe we will never be able to overcome the difficult feelings we are experiencing. To return to the guidance of Ethan Kross:

> 'Engage in mental time travel. Another way to gain distance and broaden your perspective is to think about how you'll feel a month, a year, or even longer from now. Remind yourself that you'll look back on whatever is upsetting you in the future and it'll seem much less upsetting.'

It can be very challenging to manifest empathy and positivity unless we are surrounding ourselves by these qualities at all times. It will vary for every individual, but deciding what works for you personally and being disciplined in trying to achieve that state of calm and positivity will significantly influence not only the behaviour of the teenagers in front of you, but also your own happiness levels.

CONCLUSION

There is perhaps no other age group in which communication is so complex and sensitive as it is for teenagers. This book has aimed to give space to think about how to go about that communication, and to focus on how we can hone our ability to reach our audience in a supportive and empowering way.

I hope this book has contributed positively to how we speak and act in our classrooms, and the impact it can have. If it helps teachers to be reflective and nuanced about how we use our speech and actions in the classroom, then it has been entirely worthwhile. It should help to generate classrooms in which genuine listening and learning occur, and understanding and empathy are shown – classrooms that can illuminate the very best in human nature.

There is no doubt that this process of talking to teenagers every day can be challenging.

Communication in our classrooms requires perseverance and skill. From wrestling with how to explain a challenging concept to deciding on a powerful question we might ask, the communication demands are varied and exhilarating.

As we have seen, the words we use, and how we convey them, matter immensely. The power we have to diffuse conflict, to inspire and evoke curiosity, and to forge meaningful relationships all come from the words we use.

In terms of influence and of the profound impact that communication has, no other role comes close to that of the teacher. Pausing for a moment to appreciate and be grateful for that opportunity to help shape and influence young people at a pivotal moment in their development is vital.

The scale of our impact on a daily basis is huge: we contribute to the experience of hundreds of teenagers. That should never be underestimated. The words of Alfred Adler provide a perfect point to end on:

> 'Every human being strives for significance; but people always make mistakes if they do not see that their whole significance must consist in their contribution to the lives of others.' (Adler, 1931)

I wish you a happy and fulfilling career in which you continue to contribute positively to the lives of countless teenagers. The chances are they will remember you, and what you said to them, for years to come.

A GLOSSARY OF TEACHER PHRASES

You can use this section of the book to find phrases related to the three areas that require verbal communication in the book: behaviour, the LEAP in classroom discussion, and motivation and habit-forming.

I would like to express gratitude here to all the brilliant teachers I have worked with and learned from who have contributed to this, and also to the teachers on Twitter who were kind enough to share some of their own unique phrases.

Phrases to script and teach behaviour

'In my lessons there is always a seating plan. I decide where you sit in my classroom.'

'I'm really looking forward to starting our lesson, so sit down, thank you.'

'Five: Attention on me, thanks.

Four: Excellent, thank you Julie.

Three: A couple of people still to respond.

Two: And pens down, thanks.

One: All eyes this way, thank you.'

'Settle down everyone, thank you.'

'I'm ready to start, thank you.'

'90% are beautifully focused and ready. I would like the last 10%, thank you.'

'There are three people not focused yet. I am waiting.'

'We are going to do some really good stuff in the next 50 minutes. I'd like to start.'

'I'm really excited about today's lesson because we will be…'

'You will leave here in 50 minutes with…'

'What is the purpose of today's lesson? Well…'

'I'm really disappointed folks. We have still got two really important tasks we need to complete today.'

'Why is it important that we are not fiddling with something when listening to me and each other?'

'Pens down, eyes on me, thanks.'

'Stop talking girls, thank you.'

'Should we start?' 'Yes, please.'

'Shall I hand out the books, miss?' 'Yes, please.'

'Can I share my response, sir?' 'Yes, please – that would be brilliant!'

'Thank you, John, you are being really attentive.'

'I love how carefully you are listening, Mary.'

'You are working really hard today, Aziz, thank you.'

'You thought so carefully about that, Matthew. Thank you for taking the time to do that.'

'Billy, I'd like to see you working as well as you did yesterday. Make a positive choice and stop talking, thank you.'

'Georgia, your choices today are making it difficult for you to concentrate. The work today is important and I'd really like you to have a go at it.'

'I've noticed that you haven't completed as much work as yesterday. Why is that? I'm ready to listen.'

'I've noticed you are talking again. Can you refocus? Thank you.'

'I've noticed you are a bit distracted today. I really don't want to have to keep you behind after the lesson.'

'That may be so, but right now I need you to…'

'Gentlemen, how are you getting on with the essay?'

'I'm disappointed not to see much writing. It looks to me like you are struggling to focus. Do I need to move your seats?'

'OK. I'm looking forward to coming back in 10 minutes and seeing how much you have written.'

'Can you show me how much work you have completed today?'

'Do you have any questions about the work today?'

'You have forgotten to get started with the work…'

'Pop your jacket off, thank you.'

'I did not ask you a question, so I do not need an answer.'

'This class is the highlight of my week!'

'It is so good to see you all!'

'I'm looking for those who are…' (Getting straight on with the task/ showing me great listening/working well in a team, etc.).

'Almost everyone has started the task – good. Just waiting on two more to start…'

'I will wait…'

'You were flying yesterday, Liam, and completed so many questions. What is happening today?'

'I'm really looking forward to marking your book, Georgia. Are you trying as hard as you can today?'

'I'm really looking forward to seeing you working well today, Zelda.'

'Let's have a brilliant lesson from you today, Jon.'

'Great to see you, Bob. We are going to do some great stuff today.'

'You know what the school rules are, Michael. I need your mobile to be in your bag.'

'Bob, I've noticed you have taken your phone out. You can put it away, or it will be confiscated.'

'I'm just going to make sure everyone is focused, then I will come around the room. Lovely level of focus, folks.'

'David, I was really let down by your comment to Josh earlier. I care about you doing well in my lessons and would like us to have a positive relationship.'

'If I hear that kind of comment again, I will need to have a conversation with your parents.'

'It is really important that we are respectful to each other in my classroom. If you speak to me like that again I will unfortunately need to have you removed to another classroom.'

'I really don't want to have to keep you at break, Burhana, so I need to see another paragraph written.'

'I appreciate you are upset. The reason why…'

'I can see that you disagree…'

'Hello there, it's Jimmy's English teacher. We spoke earlier this year about what a great start Jimmy has made. While I still really enjoy teaching Jimmy, some of his behavioural choices have been less positive in the last few weeks. I'd really like to explore with you how we can get back to more of what I saw at the start of the year.'

'How does Jimmy feel about his lessons?'

'Is there anything I need to know about what might be influencing Jimmy's behavioural choices in the classroom?'

'I am really grateful for your support, thank you.'

'Thank you so much for your time.'

'Please keep in touch and just send me an email if I can support in any way.'

Phrases to LEAP in classroom discussion

'That is really interesting. How did you arrive at that thinking?'

'I'm fascinated. Talk me through how you got to that answer.'

'I love that. What made you think...'

'Let me see if I am clear here...'

'Can I check to make sure I have understood you properly...'

'Can you expand on that?'

'Can you build on the detail there?'

'I think I heard you say ... is that correct?'

'Let me see if I have understood you.'

'Am I right in thinking that you...'

'What does it mean to truly listen to someone?'

'How do you know that the person is truly listening to you?'

'How do you show that you are truly listening?'

'What are ways to convey that you are listening to someone?'

'How do you feel when someone doesn't listen to you?'

'I will be saying this once...'

'You will need to listen carefully as I will not be repeating this information...'

'I'm not sure I explained that very well. Can you repeat back what you have heard?'

'Can you clarify for us what we are doing next?'

'I can see you were listening beautifully. Can you explain back what we need to do?'

'Can you just explain to me what you understand about the task...'

'There has been some brilliant listening done today, thank you, folks.'

'I love how much attention we are paying here – brilliant stuff.'

'You are focusing on me really well, thank you.'

'Thank you for some really strong examples of listening today.'

'I will be asking three different people to explain what we need to do next in 30 seconds. Can you mentally rehearse your answer please?'

'You have 30 seconds to check with your partner to make sure you understood that explanation. Then one of you will feed back.'

'What do you understand?'

'Write a summary of what you have learned into your workbook.'

'Explain what we have explored to your partner.'

'You have 30 seconds to recap on what we have covered in the past five minutes.'

'I'm fairly confident I have explained that terribly. Can you explain it to each other more effectively?'

'What exactly is a metaphor? I would like number ones to explain to number twos in 40 seconds. You must use the word "comparison".'

'Two minutes to explain to your partner what we need to do: GO!'

'What did you find helpful in today's lesson?'

'What can I do to explain things more effectively for you?'

'What helps you to understand things in a class?'

'We will be working in silence for the next 15 minutes so that we can all focus fully.'

'I'm really looking forward to reading your work, so I'm going to ask you to work in silence.'

'Why is it important we work in silence for this part of the lesson?'

'I've asked you to explore some really challenging learning today, so let's see if you can make sense of it in silence.'

'You are working beautifully, but I have noticed a couple of key points.'

'I'm really sorry to interrupt for a couple of minutes, but I would just like to clarify a couple of things...'

'Are you following your plan?'

'How much time do you have to complete this task?'

'What do you need to do more of?'

'What skills are you using?'

Phrases to drive motivation and build habits

'Well done, I like how you...'

'What is strong about that answer is...'

'I really like how you...'

'Great to see you all.'

'I have been looking forward to this lesson...'

'I'm excited about another excellent lesson with this class.'

'We've got some fantastic content to explore today. I'm so pleased to see you!'

'We don't behave like that in this classroom.'

'We are listening brilliantly, folks. Well done.'

'This is challenging, but I'm really confident we can do it.'

'We have 10 minutes to do this task.'

'We will need to think really hard for this one.'

'We have worked so well there everyone. Brilliant stuff.'

'I'm sorry, I will need to look into that – I don't know the answer.'

'Let me come back to you on that. I will look it up.'

'I know this is difficult, but I'm really confident you can manage it.'

'I believe you can give this a really good go.'

'I know you have found this difficult in the past, but you have made so much progress recently.'

'I'm so proud of the effort you have shown in that task.'

'Let's set some goals for you to work on regarding your behaviour. What do you think should be your priorities?'

'This will help you in your life because...'

'You will benefit from this because...'

'There are lots of ways you will be able to apply this...'

'Ten years in the future, you will be using this when...'

'This has a fascinating link to...'

'If you remember, we explored a similar area last term.'

'Can anyone link this to any of your other subjects?'

'We are 20 minutes in. What have we achieved from our aim today?'

'How close are we to achieving the objective for today? How do you know?'

'Let's do a learning objective check in...'

'We are going to be looking at something really fascinating today...'

'I'm confident that you will leave here today with some completely new knowledge.'

'You are going to want to share the information from this lesson with others...'

'This is going to add value to your life by...'

'This is going to be challenging, and I'm confident that...'

'What stops you?'

'What would/might happen if you did?'

'What would you rather have?'

'How would you prefer to feel?'

'What will you be doing to make sure this happens?'

'Let's think of four things we can do right now to help.'

'Talk to the person next to you for 30 seconds about this question. How would you answer it?'

'Mentally rehearse how you might answer this question. I will be asking three people to share their thinking in one minute.'

'Use your mini-whiteboard to rehearse an answer in writing. How would you answer this question?'

'No problem, take a moment to have a think and I will come back to you.'

'Let's all take a second to think about how we would answer the question.'

'It's a really difficult question. Take a few seconds to reflect on it.'

'I think you might be able to think of something...'

'Can you think of anything that might help?'

'If you did know, what might you say?'

'Which answer do you like best, and why?'

'Which answer do you think is correct? And why?'

'Phone a friend?'

'Fifty-fifty – it could be this or this. Which is right and why?'

'Who can help Joanne with the answer?'

'What did you think of that answer?'

'Was that right? If so, why?'

'Can you say more?'

'That's fine, but what else might you add to that?'

'You are on the right lines...'

'How did you get to that answer?'

'You are on the right track, but you are not there yet.'

'I can see where you are going but...'

'What you have done well is...'

'Your next steps are...'

'How are you getting on? Can you explain how you got that answer?'

'What is going well with this task?'

'Can you explain why you just did that?'

'That is a really strong answer. How did you work that out?'

BIBLIOGRAPHY

Adler, A. (1931) *What Life Should Mean To You*. Boston: Little, Brown, and company.

Aesop. (1994) *Aesop's Fables*. Ware: Wordsworth Editions.

Ainsworth, M. D. S., Blehar, M. C., Waters, E. and Wall, S. (1978) *Patterns of attachment: A psychological study of the strange situation*. Lawrence Erlbaum.

Allen, K-A. (2019) 'Making sense of belonging.' *InPsych*, 41(3): pp. 1–12.

Benson, P. L. and Bundick, M. (2015) 'Erikson and adolescent development: Contemporary views on an enduring legacy.' *Journal of Child and Youth Care Work*, 25: pp. 195–205.

Berger, R. (2022) *Models of excellence: Ron Berger explores what standards really look like*. Available at: https://modelsofexcellence.eleducation. org/resources/models-excellence-ron-berger-explores-what-standards-really-look

Blakemore, S-J. (2018) *Inventing Ourselves: The secret life of the teenage brain*. Public Affairs Books.

Blakemore, S-J., Burnett, S. and Dahl, R. E. (2010) 'The role of puberty in the developing adolescent brain.' *Human Brain Mapping*, 31(6): pp. 926–933.

Boffey, D. (2013) *Brian Cox: TV shows inspire a new generation of children to study science*. Available at: www.theguardian.com/science/2013/ may/05/brian-cox-science-tv-inspires

Boniwell, I. (2012) *Positive Psychology in a Nutshell*. 3rd edn. Maidenhead: Open University Press.

Brian, D. (1996) *Einstein: A life*. New York: John Wiley and Sons.

Brown, P. C., Roediger, H. L. and McDaniel, M. A. (2014) *Make it Stick: The science of successful learning*. Cambridge, MA: Harvard University Press.

Chua, A. (2012) *Battle Hymn of the Tiger Mother*. London: Bloomsbury Publishing.

Clear, J. (2018) *Atomic habits: An easy & proven way to build good habits & break bad ones*. New York: Avery.

Coleman, J. (2011) *The Nature of Adolescence*. Routledge.

Coleman, J. (2022) *Why I study adolescence*. Available at: www.jcoleman.co.uk/why-i-study-adolescence

Covey, S. (2004) *The 7 Habits of Highly Effective People: Restoring the character ethic*. [Rev. ed.]. New York: Free Press.

Cox, D. (2021) *The 'Curse of Knowledge' & foundational knowledge in teaching*. Available at: https://missdcoxblog.wordpress.com/2021/03/29/the-curse-of-knowledge-foundational-knowledge-in-teaching/

Cuddy, A. (2012) *Your body language may shape who you are* [video]. Available at: www.ted.com/talks/amy_cuddy_your_body_language_may_shape_who_you_are?language=en

Cuddy, A. (2015) *Presence: Bringing your boldest self to your biggest challenges*. London: Little, Brown and Company.

Dahl, R. (1975) *Danny, the Champion of the World*. Puffin Books.

De Bono, E. (1999) *Simplicity*. London: Penguin Books.

Deci, E. and Ryan, R. (1985) *Intrinsic Motivation and Self-Determination in Human Behaviour*. Plenum Press.

Didau, D. (2015) *What If Everything You Knew About Education Was Wrong?* Carmarthen: Crown House Publishing.

Didau, D. (2019) *Making Kids Cleverer*. Carmarthen: Crown House Publishing.

Didau, D. and Rose, N. (2016) *What Every Teacher Needs to Know About Psychology*. Woodbridge: John Catt Educational.

Dix, P. (2010) *How to manage behaviour in the classroom.* Available at: www.theguardian.com/society/joepublic/2010/feb/09/pupil-behaviour-management-tips

Dix, P. (2017) *When the Adults Change, Everything Changes: Seismic shifts in school behaviour.* Carmarthen: Independent Thinking Press.

Duckworth, A. (2016) *Grit: The power of passion and perseverance.* London: Scribner.

Dweck, C. (2007) *Mindset: The new psychology of success.* New York: Ballantine.

EEF. (2021) *Improving behaviour in schools.* Available at: https://educationendowmentfoundation.org.uk/public/files/Publications/Behaviour/EEF_Improving_behaviour_in_schools_Report.pdf

Fiorella, L. (2020) 'The science of habit and its implications for student learning and well-being. *Educational Psychology Review,* 32(3): pp. 603–625.

Fletcher-Wood, H. (2016) *Ticked off: Checklists for teachers, students, school leaders.* Carmarthen: Crown House Publishing.

Fogg, B. J. (2020) *Tiny Habits.* Houghton Mifflin Harcourt.

Frank, A. (2012) *The Diary of a Young Girl: The definitive edition.* Penguin.

Fredrickson, B. (2009) *Positivity: Groundbreaking research to release your inner optimist and thrive.* Oneworld publications.

Goleman, D. (1996) *Emotional Intelligence: Why it can matter more than IQ.* London: Bloomsbury.

Goodenow, C. and Grady, K. E. (1993) 'The relationship of school belonging and friends' values to academic motivation among urban adolescent students.' *The Journal of Experimental Education,* 62(1): pp. 60–71.

Hall, D. (2013) *Brief letters.* Available at: www.theguardian.com/theguardian/2013/jan/04/pickles-in-a-sweat

Harlow, E. (2018) *Attachment theory in schools.* Available at: www.headteacher-update.com/best-practice-article/attachment-theory-in-schools/167068/

Harter, S. (1990) 'Issues in the assessment of the self-concept of children and adolescents.' In: La Greca, A. M., (Ed.) *Through the Eyes of the Child: Obtaining self-reports from children and adolescents.* Needham Heights: Allyn & Bacon, pp. 292–325.

Harvard Medical School. (2022) *Is it too late to save your posture?* Available at: www.health.harvard.edu/staying-healthy/is-it-too-late-to-save-your-posture

Hattie, J. and Timperley, H. (2007) 'The power of feedback.' *Review of Educational Research*, 77(1): pp. 81–112.

Hattie, J. and Yates, G. C. R. (2013) *Visible Learning and the Science of How We Learn.* Oxon: Routledge.

Heath, C. and Heath, D. (2006) *The Curse of Knowledge.* Available at: https://hbr.org/2006/12/the-curse-of-knowledge

Heath, C. and Heath, D. (2007) *Made to Stick: Why some ideas take hold and others come unstuck.* London: Random House Business Books.

Hendrick, C. and Macpherson, R. (2017) *What Does This Look Like in the Classroom?* Woodbridge: John Catt Educational.

Hunley, S. (2017) *Problematic smartphone use and its relationship to anxiety and depression.* Available at: www.anxiety.org/smartphone-use-and-its-relationship-to-anxiety-and-depression

Hysing, M., Pallesen, S., Stormark, K. M., Jakobsen, R., Lundervold, A. J. and Sivertsen, B. (2015) 'Sleep and use of electronic devices in adolescence: Results from a large population-based study.' *BMJ Open*, 5(1): e006748.

Innerdrive. (2022) *Managing mobile phones.* Available at: www.innerdrive.co.uk/mobile-phone-management/

Jensen, F. E. (2015) *The Teenage Brain.* Harper.

Kline, N. (1999) *Time to Think: Listening to ignite the human mind.* London: Octopus Publishing Group.

Knight, R. (2017) *UK adults smile 11 times every day – more than 232,000 times over their lifetime.* Available at: https://swnsdigital.com/uk/2017/10/the-average-uk-adult-smiles-11-times-every-day-more-than-232000-times-over-their-lifetime/

Koestenbaum, P. (2000) *Talking intelligently about leadership.* Available at: www.pib.net/articles/anxiety.htm

Kreber, C., Klampfleitner, M., McCune, V., Bayne, S., and Knottenbelt, M. (2007) 'What do you mean by "authentic"? A comparative review of the literature on conceptions of authenticity in teaching.' *Adult Education Quarterly*, 58(1): pp. 22–44.

Kross, E. (2021) *Chatter: The voice in our head, why it matters, and how to harness it.* New York: Crown.

Lee, H. (2010) *To Kill a Mockingbird.* London: Arrow Books.

Lemov, D. (2010) *Teach Like a Champion.* San Francisco: John Wiley & Sons.

Lemov, D. (2014) *Teach Like a Champion 2.0.* San Francisco: John Wiley & Sons.

Lemov, D. (2016) *On 'please' and 'thank you'.* Available at: https://teachlikeachampion.org/blog/on-please-and-thank-you/

Lemov, D. (2018) *Teaching the art of listening in the age of me, me, me.* Available at: www.tes.com/magazine/archive/teaching-art-listening-age-me-me-me

Lemov, D. (2021) *What I told my kids about doing well in college/university.* Available at: https://teachlikeachampion.org/blog/what-i-told-my-kids-about-doing-well-in-college-university/

Levine, A. and Heller, R. S. F. (2019) *Attached.* Bluebird.

Lightfoot, C. (1997) *The culture of adolescent risk-taking.* New York: Guilford Press.

Lovell, O. (2020) *Cognitive Load Theory in action.* Available at: www.ldaustralia.org/app/uploads/2021/03/Lovell-Cognitive-Load-Theory-in-action.pdf

Main, M. and Solomon, J. (1986) 'Discovery of an insecure-disorganized/disoriented attachment pattern.' In: Yogman, M. W. and Brazelton, T. B. (eds.), *Affective development in infancy* (pp. 95–124). Norwood, NJ: Ablex.

Maricchiolo, F., Bonaiuto, M. and Gnisci, A. (2005) 'Hand gestures in speech: Studies of their roles in social interaction.' University of Rome.

Marland, M. (1993) *The Craft of the Classroom*. Heinemann.

Mccrea, P. (2020) *Motivated Teaching*. CreateSpace Independent Publishing Platform.

Mehrabian, A. (1972) *Nonverbal communication*. Piscataway, NJ: Aldine Transaction.

Mehrabian, A. (1981) *Silent Messages: Implicit communication of emotions and attitudes*. 2nd edn. Belmont, California: Wadsworth Publishing Company.

Murphy, K. (2017) *Yes, it's your parents' fault*. Available at: www.nytimes.com/2017/01/07/opinion/Sunday/yes-its-your-parents-fault.html

Murphy, K. (2020) *You're Not Listening: What you're missing and why it matters*. Harvill Secker.

Myatt, M. (2016) *Hopeful Schools: Building humane communities*. Mary Myatt Learning Limited.

Nuthall, G. (2007) *The Hidden Lives of Learners*. Wellington: NZCER Press.

Obama, B. (2008) *Barack Obama's New Hampshire Primary Speech*. Available at: www.nytimes.com/2008/01/08/us/politics/08text-obama.html

Parker, R. (2018) *Student behaviour, motivation and the potential of attachment-aware schools to redefine the landscape*. Available at: www.bera.ac.uk/blog/student-behaviour-motivation-and-the-potential-of-attachment-aware-schools-to-redefine-the-landscape

Pearce, C. (2016) *A Short Introduction to Attachment and Attachment Disorder*. London: Jessica Kingsley Publishers.

Pinker, S. (2015) *The Sense of Style: The thinking person's guide to writing in the 21st century*. Penguin.

Quigley, A. (2013) *Explanations: Top 10 teaching tips*. Available at: www.theconfidentteacher.com/2013/05/explanations-top-ten-teaching-tips/

Quigley, A. (2018) *Closing the Vocabulary Gap*. Routledge.

Riches, A. (2019) *Get out from behind the desk.* Available at: www.sec-ed. co.uk/best-practice/get-out-from-behind-the-desk/

Rogers, B. (2007) *Behaviour Management: A whole-school approach.* London: Paul Chapman Publishing.

Rogers, C. R. (1980) *A Way of Being.* Boston, MA: Houghton Mifflin.

Scrivener, J. (2011) *Learning Teaching: The essential guide to English language teaching.* MacMillan Books for Teachers.

Seligman, M. E. P. (1998) *Learned Optimism.* New York: Pocket Books.

Seneca, L. A. (1969) *Letters from a Stoic: Epistulae Morales Ad Lucilium.* Penguin Books.

Shakespeare, W. (1992) *Macbeth.* Wordsworth Editions.

Sherrington, T. (2017) *The Learning Rainforest: Great teaching in real classrooms.* Woodbridge: John Catt Educational Ltd.

Sherrington, T. (2021) *Five Ways to: Build Fluency.* Available at: https:// teacherhead.com/2021/12/06/five-ways-to-build-fluency/

Shrestha, P. (2017) *Drive reduction theory.* Available at: www.psychestudy. com/general/motivation-emotion/drive-reduction-theory

Siegel, D. (2014) *Brainstorm: The power and purpose of the teenage brain.* Penguin.

Sinek, S. (2011) *Start with Why: How great leaders inspire everyone to take action.* London: Portfolio Penguin.

Sleep Foundation. (2022a) *Teens and sleep.* Available at: www. sleepfoundation.org/teens-and-sleep

Sleep Foundation. (2022b) *Screen time and insomnia: What it means for teens.* Available at: www.sleepfoundation.org/teens-and-sleep/screen-time-and-insomnia-for-teens

Stanier, M. (2020) *Advice Trap.* Page Two Books.

Steinberg, L. (2012) *Should the science of adolescent brain development inform public policy?* Available at: https://issues.org/steinberg-science-adolescent-teenage-brain-policy/

Sweller, J. (1988) 'Cognitive load during problem solving: Effects on learning.' *Cognitive Science*, 12(2): pp. 257–285.

Sweller, J. (2016) 'Cognitive load theory, evolutionary educational psychology, and instructional design.' In D. C. Geary and D. B. Berch (eds.), *Evolutionary perspectives on child development and education* (pp. 291–306). Springer International Publishing/Springer Nature.

Sweller, J., van Merrienboer, J. and Paas, F. (1998) 'Cognitive architecture and instructional design.' *Educational Psychology Review*, 10: pp. 251–296.

The Attachment Research Community. (n. d.) *What is attachment?* Available at: https://the-arc.org.uk/what-is-attachment

Thom, J. (2020) *A Quiet Education*. Woodbridge: John Catt Educational.

Thoreau, H. D. (1908) *Walden: or, Life in the woods*. London: J. M. Dent.

Weiner, B. (1980) *Human Motivation*. New York: Holt, Rinehart and Winston.

Wiliam, D. (2017) [Twitter] 26 January. Available at: https://twitter.com/dylanwiliam/status/824682504602943489?lang=en-GB

Willingham, D. T. (2005) 'How praise can motivate – or stifle.' *American Educator*, 29(4): pp. 23–27.

Willingham, D. T. (2010) *Why Don't Students Like School?* Jossey-Bass.

ACKNOWLEDGEMENTS

Thank you first to Fiona for all her love, support and encouragement. I keep saying this will be the last book, but we probably both know that isn't true! Our two wee boys, Matthew and Christopher, deserve a thank you for brining utter joy to our lives. Any rambling sections or mistakes, however, are entirely their fault: either the result of sleep deprivation or writing in front of *Peppa Pig*.

As always, a huge thank you to my mum and dad for inspiring me to choose a career in teaching and for their encouragement and support. Thank you to my brothers, Fergus and Stephen, for helping every step of the way.

Thank you to Natasha Gladwell at John Catt Educational, whose incisive editing and attention to detail have vastly improved this book. Her unremitting positivity, patience and enthusiasm has been hugely appreciated throughout the process.

I have been lucky to work with lots of brilliant teachers and leaders, whose ideas and wonderful communication styles I have pinched for this book – thank you. I have amazing colleagues (and students!) now at Edinburgh Napier University, who I feel lucky to work with and learn from.

Thank you to all the wonderful teenagers who contributed to this book. Hundreds of you either filled in the survey or took the time to speak to me, and the sensitivity and depth of reflection you demonstrated was so impressive and mature. Your education matters deeply, and I hope this book might help teachers provide the best possible support to you.

I never take for granted how fortunate I am to write, both in enjoying the process and in being able to share it with others. Thank you again to

Alex, Jonathan and all the team at John Catt Educational for making that possible.